BLACK SEA

Macedonia

Thrace

Byzantium

Abdera

Pella

◇Thasos

Phrygia

Troy

AEGEAN SEA

Pergamon

Sardis

Lesbos

Lydia

Chios

Smyrna

phi

Chalcis

Thebes

Eretria

Ephesos

Caria

Corinth

Samos

Priene

Athens

Miletus

Aegina

Delos

Lycia

os

Peros

Naxos

ta

Knidos

Rhodes

Melos

Cyprus

Syria

Crete

Knossos

Gortyn

COLLECTING
GREEK
ANTIQUITIES

COLLECTING GREEK ANTIQUITIES

HERBERT HOFFMANN

Introduction by
JOHN D. COONEY
Cleveland Museum of Art

A Chapter on Coins by
HERBERT A. CAHN

Clarkson N. Potter, Inc./Publisher NEW YORK
DISTRIBUTED BY CROWN PUBLISHERS, INC.

Library of Congress Catalog Card Number: 69-13401

Printed in the United States of America

Published simultaneously in Canada by General Publishing Company Limited

First Edition

Designed by Leonard Cascioli

Preface

The demand for a collector's manual in the field of ancient art has become acute in recent years. Though there are many histories of Greek art, there has never been a practical work for the collector. The aim of this book is to provide such a guide.

The illustrations in the book consist of photographs and drawings. By and large, the photographs are of objects of above-average importance and are intended to act as criteria for the quality of Greek antiquities. Pieces of lesser importance have been deliberately selected for the line drawings. Line drawings have the advantage of generalizing the objects while emphasizing their type, and the lesser pieces are instructive "collector's items."

The two principal collections of Greek antiquities in the United States, those of the Museum of Fine Arts, Boston, and of the Metropolitan Museum, New York, are heavily represented in the illustrations for obvious reason: the two museums must of necessity serve as points of departure for any serious American collecting effort in the field. Hamburg's Museum für Kunst und Gewerbe—the author's institution—has also provided many illustrations.

I have enjoyed the active and moral support of a great many friends and colleagues while writing this book. In particular I should like to thank A. Greifenhagen of the Staatliche Museen, Berlin (West), R. A. Higgins of the British Museum, and H. Sichtermann of the German Archaeological Institute, Rome, for their help with photographs. The Curator of the Classical Department at the Museum of Fine Arts, Boston, C. C. Vermeule, generously scheduled special photography for use in this publication. In addition the following curators, collectors, and dealers have very kindly contributed photographs of and/or information concerning objects in their possession or care:

D. Ahrens (Munich), J. Ch. Balty (Brussels), H. Bloesch (Zurich), R. Boehringer (Geneva), E. Borowski (Basel), B. V. Bothmer (Brooklyn), H. A. Cahn (Basel), W. H. Catling (Oxford), J. Cooney (Cleveland), S. Doeringer (Cambridge), G. Dontas (Athens), C. Dunant (Geneva), U. Gehrig (Berlin), M. Gjodesen (Copenhagen), G. M. A. Hanfmann (Cambridge), H. von Heintze (Rome), HRH Prince Philipp of Hesse (Adolphseck), D. Hill (Baltimore), I. and H. Jucker (Bern), H. W. Keiser (Oldenburg), J. J. Klejman (New York), E. Kofler-Truniger (Lucerne), N. Leipen (Toronto), R. Lullies (Kassel), D. and J. de Ménil (Houston), A. Moretti (Bellinzona), D. and J. Nash (New York), P. Near (Richmond), G. Ortiz (Geneva), A. Peredolskaya (Leningrad), H. and L. Pomerance (New York), G. M. A. Richter (Rome), E. Rowlett (Columbia), E. and N. Schimmel (New York), Mr. and Mrs. G. Schindler (New York), W. Schröder (Stuttgart), T. Sulley (Indianapolis), J. Ternbach (New York), E. L. B. Terrace (Boston), J. Thimme (Karlsruhe), P. Truitt (Boston), K. Vierneisel (Munich), H. Vollmoeller (Zurich), H. Wahl (Pforzheim), F. M. Watkins (New Haven).

I am extremely grateful to my colleague John Boardman for reading my manuscript and saving me from a number of errors.

The translation, from the German, of Herbert Cahn's chapter on Greek coins is my own.

With the exception of the drawings of Greek sculpture, which are by Carl Helmut Steckner, all drawings are by Martina Naubereit of the Römisch-Germanisches Zentralmuseum, Mainz, to whose skill and diligence I am indebted.

Jane West edited my manuscript and made many suggestions for its improvement; Sharon Nathanson dealt with the arduous task of assembling the photographic material. To both, the author wishes to express his sincere gratitude.

Contents

Introduction

Today, a Baedeker in any field of art collecting must be a practical work. There would be little point, for example, in a guidebook outlining the fine points of Sumerian sculpture or Elamite works of art, or one attempting to guide a potential collector in appreciating the finer points of various Botticelli paintings. While these hypothetical volumes could be fascinating as surveys of great achievements or dull as mere vehicles of learning, they would be of little practical use, as all three fields mentioned are, for the foreseeable future at least, closed or exhausted. The practicality of this book is that it expertly guides a potential collector in the one ancient field in which, surprisingly, material still appears in adequate quantity to make collecting possible and to maintain the collector's interest. With the ambiguous exception of the Iranian field, no other ancient culture is so well represented on the international art market. Occasionally a stray Mesopotamian object appears from an old collection, but it would be impossible today to form even a small collection from that interesting area. In the Egyptian field, once seemingly inexhaustible (and, potentially, it still is), very little that is fine now reaches the market. It would be impossible at this late date to form a choice collection in that field.

In contrast to these archaeological famines, the Greek field, or, in more general terms, the classical art market, flourishes with a relative wealth of material. Indeed, most important museums and collectors are annually offered more desirable classical objects than they can afford to buy, and that statement includes some rather wealthy institutions. Relatively little of this material comes from Greece proper, but rather from the innumerable colonies spread throughout the western Asiatic mainland and the entire Mediterranean basin. To some extent each colony developed its own style, which is one explanation of the variety of material available to the collector. And the current choice available to a collector of classical art is still varied. Painted vases are now available in such quantity that it would easily be possible to form an important collection of them— a costly undertaking, doubtless, but an entirely feasible one. A realistic collector could probably not hope to gather a selection of fifth-century marbles; but within the last decade several fine archaic marbles have been on the market, and choice examples of the fourth century are not to be disdained. They are frequently found. Bronzes, jewelry, coins, and similar small-scale objects of the very highest quality constantly come on the market and are a delight to the knowledgeable collector.

And there is an important point: a knowledgeable collector. How is that esoteric state reached? Using this book doubtless will help, but no degree of mere reading will develop a feeling for quality, the ultimate achievement of any serious collector, professional or amateur. Sometimes it is called "taste," a quality not infrequently lacking in very learned scholars and even among museum men, to the great detriment of their collections. Interest is basic to its development, and perhaps an unusual degree of sensitivity must be inherent. Given these characteristics, the sole path to an appreciation of quality is the seeing, preferably the handling, of innumerable objects within the collector's field. This is not an easy undertaking, but neither is it an impossible one, assuming that the collector has easy access to a metropolitan center. If, however, he is in a provincial area, the problem is hopeless. There are numerous excellent public collections of Greek art in this country that should be haunted by every serious collector, who should see their major pieces again and again. The exhibitions prior to auction sales, even if the objects are of minor importance, provide another opportunity to see fresh material.

The most practical advice that can be extended to a beginning collector is to make friends with a dealer or, better, with several of them, all of them preferably knowledgeable and important. Indeed, this is basic for any success as a collector. Today, the market belongs to the seller. The day of imposing galleries with large stocks of antiquities, which, in New York, Paris, and London, were conventional until shortly after the last war, is gone forever. In those days the market belonged to the collector. Today, the important dealers show their fine pieces only to a handful of important buyers who have the knowledge and means to buy. But the same dealers will, if they know a collector is discriminating and deeply interested, show their fine things to him for their mutual pleasure, even if there is no possibility that the collector could make the purchase. After all, dealers are human. They enjoy having visits from collectors; they love to talk shop and to swap stories—making a purchase is by no means necessary. In the long run, the relationship will pay dividends and, what is more important, will make collecting much more enjoyable.

Forming a collection makes formidable demands on the individual, financially, intellectually, and emotionally, but I have known very few individuals to abandon it voluntarily once embarked on the venture. It has a curious fascination that defies analysis. Although I have known and still know many collectors in many fields, I have never identified any common denominator among them with the possible exception that women are rarely collectors. In recent years in New York one does find the team of the young married couple as collectors, but even here the initiative seems to be with the man. But let the psychiatrists ponder that problem.

If, after reading this book, you are impelled to become a collector of Greek art, there is still another quality you must possess. It is essential to have something of the gambler in you; and if you possess a sense of humor in addition, it will help. For if, on the basis of this guide and nothing else, you venture to make a purchase, the chances are that your first purchase will be a fake (mine was; rather a costly one) or a run-of-the-mill mediocrity. Which of the two is the lesser evil I still don't know. Indeed, it is probably impossible to form an extensive collection in any field without making mistakes of judgment either as to quality or authenticity. If anyone tells you he has never made a mistake in collecting, either he is, to phrase it gently, playing with fact or has had very limited experience. A well-known museum man, no longer with us, always stated that he had never made a mistake in a long career. Alas, he simply did not acknowledge his mistakes—a simple if childish solution.

Amateurs also tend to be miscellaneous in their acquisitions, which, though understandable, is a state the serious collector must outgrow. Lacking unlimited resources and space, the collector, once over the elementary stages of the game, should carefully consider the advisability of concentrating his purchases within a particular class of objects, period of time, or otherwise limiting his collecting activities so that the collection will achieve a definite and individual identity. In a very general way this could be attained by following the Cleveland policy of buying in any field only those objects believed to be outstanding examples of their kind—virtually the policy I followed in forming the Egyptian collection in Brooklyn, where I bought only pieces I believed to be works of art (and the mixture of archaeology with art is why so many Egyptian collections lack distinction). Avoid, as you would sin, the purchase of the typical example, the good specimen, and so on. Or, what is more fun for the private collector, concentrate in a particular class of objects. Several distinguished private collections have been developed around classical bronzes. In concentrating one's collection, not only does the collection gain but, inevitably, the collector himself begins to know something of his field, and it has happened that he may even become something of an authority in his subject. Collecting is much better sport when the collector really knows what he is doing. The field of concentration must be determined by personal predilection and what is available, or likely to be available, on the current market.

Even within a field of specialization a secondary policy can be imposed. That is, to limit the size of the collection to an arbitrary number, say fifty or a hundred, preferably less, objects. Once the maximum has been reached, the following purchase will force the decision of which piece to eliminate from the collection. By this stage the collector should have sufficient discrimination to make a sound choice. A collection developed in this manner would, almost certainly, culminate in one of some distinction. In any case, whatever the system used, every collection needs weeding out and strengthening if it is going to be a good one. That goal takes effort, money, and knowledge, with a seasoning of luck.

JOHN D. COONEY

Cleveland Museum of Art

COLLECTING
GREEK
ANTIQUITIES

Fig. 1. Black basalt head of a Negro boy. Alexandrian. Late Hellenistic, 1st half, 1st century B.C. Museum für Kunst und Gewerbe, Hamburg. Inv. no. 1961,1. *Photograph: F. Hewicker.*

1

Marble Sculpture

Only museums and a handful of private collectors collect ancient sculpture today. Not that they are not available, but, by and large, the general prejudice against ancient sculpture today is that it is "too large to fit into an apartment." And the great majority of modern collectors are apartment dwellers. Earlier in this century, and in the last, private sculpture collections were more plentiful.

Here, then, is where great bargains still remain to be made. As old collections are broken up, more and more classical sculptures become available. In addition, fresh finds continuously appear, despite official bans forbidding their export. The museums are, generally speaking, interested only in "important pieces"—in major monuments of lapidary art. Classical marble sculptures are consequently lower in price today than ever before. To give an example: The head of a laughing Negro in black basalt (Fig. 1), a rare example of Alexandrian "genre" art dating from the first century B.C., was purchased a few years ago by a museum on the open market for less than the price of a small bronze by Henry Moore, such as are cast and sold in several identical examples.

1

HISTORICAL DEVELOPMENT

Cycladic Idols

The above reference to bargains, it must be admitted, does not apply to Cycladic idols—the object, presently, of a full-fledged collecting mania. Their success is easy to understand: their abstract forms appear made to order for contemporary taste. Whereas during the latter nineteenth century the "Graecian" creations of Canova and Thorvaldsen set the canon as to what is art, today our eyes have been schooled by Arp, Picasso, and Brancusi.

Being so greatly in demand, Cycladic sculptures have been known to fetch

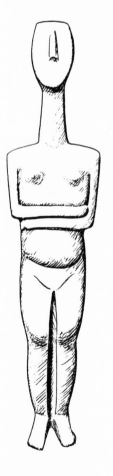

Cycladic marble idols

in the tens of thousands of dollars (depending on their size). A recent exhibition of Cycladic art in Manhattan was sold out a few days after it opened. The market in Cycladic idols, like that in modern art, is, of course, a controlled one; it is manipulated by a few dealers who have cornered the supply.

Seen historically, Cycladic idols are not Greek in the narrow sense of the word. They were produced in the Aegean islands over four thousand years ago that is to say, centuries before the arrival of the first Greek-speaking tribes. The influence of these sculptures on Greek art was nonexistent or negligible; abstraction per se held little appeal to the Greek aesthetic sense.

The most common type of Cycladic idol (Figs. 2a, 2b) represents a long-necked sloping-shouldered woman standing feet together, toes pointed downward, her arms crossed under her breasts. These figures are elegantly designed: both their heads and bodies are subtly S-shaped, discreetly streamlined. They impart a grand impression even when seen from behind. Seen from the front and side, the heads are U-shaped and tilted slightly backward. (In one variety, from Asia Minor, the heads are tilted back almost at a right angle [Fig. 3]). Usually the nose, prominent and wedge-shaped, is the only feature of the face that is represented by sculptural means; the mouth and eyes were generally shown in red and black paint, traces of which sometimes survive. The generally accepted view is that the Cycladic idols represent fertility goddesses, and the emphasis placed on breasts and genitalia would seem to favor this interpretation.

Simplicity and abstraction keynote the forms, these elements being dictated by the primitive means at the artist's disposal, for these sophisticated sculptures were carved before the invention of metal tools. Their flat contours were painstakingly abraded, employing locally available vulcanic emery, water, and a sharp-edged rubbing stone. The idols are found on nearly every island of the Cycladic archipelago, as well as on the mainland of Asia Minor. Their dimensions vary considerably—from circa six inches to four feet and over. The large and very expressive heads in the collections of Alistair Bradley Martin (Figs. 4a, 4b) and Norbert Schimmel (Figs. 5a, 5b) in New York undoubtedly belong to idols of the monumental variety.

It is generally assumed that the simpler and more abstract varieties, such as the "violin-shaped" idols (Colorplate 1), are early, whereas the more advanced creations, such as the two superposed figures (Fig. 6) and the harp player (Fig. 7) in the Karlsruhe Museum or the flute player in Athens, are late—perhaps as "recent" as 2000 B.C. There is, however, little evidence for precise chronology.

Figs. 2a, 2b. Marble female idol from Paros. Early Cycladic period, circa 3500 - 3000 B.C. Museum für Kunst und Gewerbe, Hamburg. Inv. no. 1927,135. *Museum photograph.*

Fig. 3. Female idol ("moon-gazer" type). Said to have been found at Kutcherdileryaila in southwest Anatolia together with two other examples, in the Schimmel Collection and in the Museum of Primitive Art, New York, respectively. Late 3rd millennium B.C. G. Schindler Collection, New York.
Photograph: courtesy of the owner.

Figs. 4a, 4b. Head and neck from a Cycladic idol. Third to 2nd millennium B.C. The height (12¼ inches) is unusual. Alastair B. Martin Collection, New York.
Photograph: courtesy of the Brooklyn Museum.

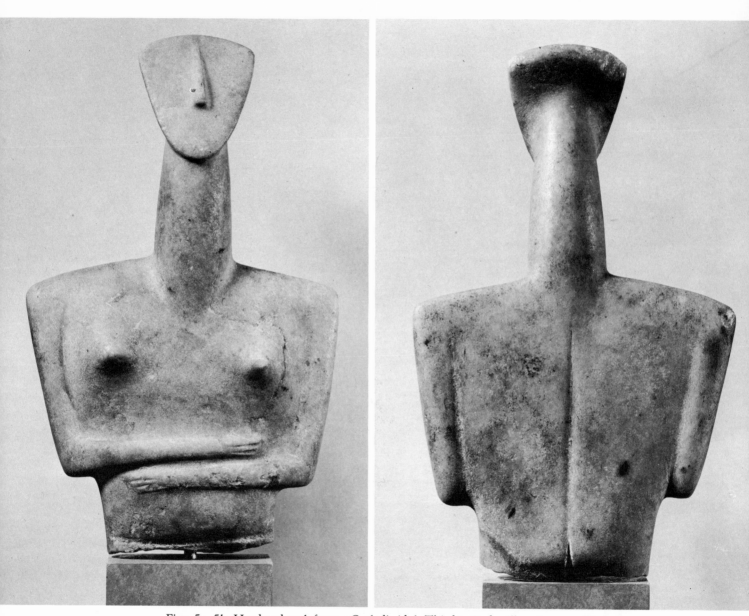

Figs. 5a, 5b. Head and neck from a Cycladic idol. Third to 2nd millennium B.C. Norbert
Schimmel Collection, New York.
Photograph: courtesy of the owner.

Fig. 7. Harp player from Thera. Cycladic, 3rd to 2nd millennium B.C. Badisches Landesmuseum, Karlsruhe. Inv. no. B 8640. A similar harpist is in the Metropolitan Museum of Art, New York.
Museum photograph.

Fig. 6. Two superposed figures. Cycladic, 3rd to 2nd millennium B.C. Badisches Landesmuseum, Karlsruhe. Inv. no. B 839.
Museum photograph.

Archaic Sculpture

Monumental stone carving does not begin in Greece until the end of the seventh century B.C., the beginning of the Archaic period of Greek art. Contact with the venerable civilizations of Egypt and the ancient Near East seems to have provided the catalyst that launched Greek sculpture on its course. Unfortunately, we must skip over this important period lightly, for, by and large, Archaic marble sculpture must be considered out of reach of all but the wealthiest of private collectors. Relatively little marble sculpture was produced during the early period, and when an Archaic Greek statue or relief does occasionally appear on the antiquities market, it is competed for by museums and leading collectors the world over.

From time to time a lucky find can be made. A good example is the fragmentary head of an Attic *kouros* (Greek youth) (Fig. 9)—magnificent in spite of its mutilation—recently acquired by a London collector. The forms of this work, which dates from the middle of the sixth century B.C., are cubic and severe. The youth's large eyes bulge markedly and his hair is rendered in a pattern of neatly stylized curls. The crisp yet solid structure of the head is filled with energy; compact form (suggesting strength and vitality) is combined with subtle elegance and charm.

Another important find made by a private collector in recent years is the unfinished head broken from an Eastern Greek marble relief dating from the second half of the sixth century B.C. This rare Archaic marble turned up on the Paris market (Fig. 10). The head of a *kore* in Cleveland (Fig. 8) takes us into the fifth century and the transition to the Classical period of Greek sculpture.

Fig. 8. Head of a *kore* (worshiper). Transitional style, circa 480-470 B.C. Cleveland Museum of Art. Acc. no. 24.538. Gift from J. H. Wade.
Museum photograph.

Fig. 9. Fragmentary head of a kouros. Archaic Greek, 3rd quarter, 6th century B.C. Private collection.
Photograph: courtesy of the owner.

Fig. 10. Unfinished male head, broken from a relief. Said to be from Turkey. Eastern Greek. Last quarter, 6th century B.C. Norbert Schimmel Collection, New York. A second head, presumably from the same monument, has been acquired by the Museum of Fine Arts, Boston.
Photograph: courtesy of the owner.

Sculpture of the Classical Age (fifth and fourth centuries B.C.)

The beginning of the fifth century B.C. marks the dawn of the "Golden Age" of Greek art. The marble sculptures of this period fall into two groups: tomb sculptures and public monuments. We shall take up the tomb sculptures first.

During the fifth and fourth centuries B.C. Athens was the leading Greek center for the production of carved gravestones, although it was not until the fourth century that they were created in large numbers (owing chiefly to the ascendancy of a middle-class clientele). In 317 B.C. and again in 307 B.C. sumptuous tombs were forbidden by decrees aimed at the suppression of luxury, thereby providing a *terminus ante quem* for the majority of extant grave reliefs.

The most common form of Attic tomb monument has the shape of a *naiskos,* or small shrine. Sometimes the pediment is surmounted by the figure of a siren, the bird of death, sometimes by a floral acroterium. Beneath the pediment there is generally a relief showing the dead person with idealized, one might say depersonalized, features. Sometimes several figures are shown, and in the larger and more important monuments these figures are carved nearly fully in the round. The scene most commonly represented is one of leavetaking, with the deceased holding his most precious possession, perhaps a pet. Often the dead person is seated pensively in a chair being bidden farewell by members of the family. One example shows a seated woman clasping the hand of a standing man, evidently her husband (Fig. 11); another shows a woman receiving a small casket from a servant (Fig. 12). The name of the person represented is frequently cut into the pediment above the relief, as on our gravestones today. Where no carved inscription is visible, the name may have been added in paint. This is frequently the case with the smaller, less important, *stelae.* Often, such painted inscriptions can still be read with the aid of an ultraviolet lamp.

There are other varieties of Attic grave monuments, including sculptures in the round. For a fuller discussion, the reader is referred to the Bibliography. We shall mention only the marble *lekythoi,* gravestones in the shape of the oil containers that were deposited at the tomb. These exist in a variety of sizes, and, like the pottery versions (cf. pp. 83-138) they imitate, they are generally decorated with leavetaking scenes (Figs. 13a, 13b).

Naturally, other areas of Greece also produced funerary sculptures, although not in such great quantities as Attica. *Boeotian stelae* are recognizable by their relatively coarse workmanship and by their dark reddish-brown surface (caused

Athenian grave relief, *Hamburg*

Fig. 11. Grave relief of Lysistrate. Attic. Middle of 4th century B.C. Courtesy of the Trustees, Metropolitan Museum of Art, New York. Acc. no. 06.287. Rogers Fund, 1906.
Museum photograph.

Fig. 12. Grave relief: "Woman and Servant." Attic. Circa 400 B.C. Courtesy of the Trustees, Metropolitan Museum of Art, New York. Acc. no. 36.11.1. Fletcher Fund, 1936.
Museum photograph.

Figs. 13a, 13b. Marble lekythos. Inscribed with the names Timagora, Aion, and Smikros. Second half, 4th century B.C. Museum für Kunst und Gewerbe, Hamburg. Inv. no. M 865.
Museum photograph.

Fig. 14. Relief representing a seated male figure (Dionysos?) holding an unidentified object, perhaps a staff. From Thasos. Late Archaic, circa 500-480 B.C. Norbert Schimmel Collection, New York.
Photograph: courtesy of the owner.

by the rich supply of iron in the Boeotian soil). A rare example of a grave relief from the northern Greek island of Thasos is in a New York private collection (Fig. 14). It represents a man, draped in a himation, seated to the right on a round-backed chair similar to the marble chairs reserved for high dignitaries in the Greek theatres. He has a carefully groomed beard, and holds an unidentified object in his hand. The small size of the relief has led some scholars to think that it may be a votive dedication to a divinity—perhaps Dionysos. It dates from the early fifth century B.C.

Tarentum in South Italy was an important overseas center for funerary sculpture in the second half of the fourth century B.C. In the Tarentine region entire tombs were decorated with relief carvings, and pieces occasionally appear on the market. The material is native limestone; it is soft and brown when freshly cut, but hardens and lightens as it ages. Typical examples are the battling warriors in Cleveland (Fig. 15) and the small limestone Amazon in Adolph-

Fig. 15. Limestone relief representing two battling warriors (Hermes and Ares?). Tarentine. Late 4th - 3rd centuries B.C. Cleveland Museum of Art. Acc. no. 27.436. Purchase from the J. H. Wade Fund.
Museum photograph.

seck (Fig. 16), fragments of battle scenes. Small grave reliefs continued to be carved in Greece during the Hellenistic and Roman periods. The late reliefs from Ionia, mostly with the standing figure of a woman, occasionally become available, and some are of quite good quality.

Fragments of grave reliefs can be eloquent works of art, and certainly deserve to be collected. Thus, for example, a sensitively carved female hand holding an alabastrum (Fig. 17), in Boston, is probably part of a relief of the com-

Fig. 16. Fragment of a limestone relief representing a fleeing girl, perhaps a Niobid. Tarentine. Late 4th - 3rd centuries B.C. Collection of HRH Prince Philipp von Hesse, Schloss Fasanerie, Adolphseck near Fulda.
Photograph: Staatliche Kunstsammlungen, Kassel.

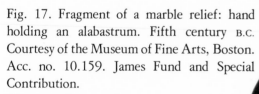

Fig. 17. Fragment of a marble relief: hand holding an alabastrum. Fifth century B.C. Courtesy of the Museum of Fine Arts, Boston. Acc. no. 10.159. James Fund and Special Contribution.
Museum photograph.

mon "farewell" type (the seated woman holding a favorite possession). The piece dates from the Transitional period, circa 490 - 480 B.C. The bearded head in Hamburg, illustrated in our drawing, formed part of a mid-fourth-century funerary monument.

The development of public sculpture was dominated during this period by artists whose names ring as familiar as those of Donatello and Michelangelo. They are Myron, Phidias, and Polyclitus for the fifth century; Scopas, Praxiteles, and Lysippus for the fourth. The reader may wonder how these masters can be relevant to a book on collecting when, as everyone knows, hardly an example of their work survives. This brings us to Roman copies. The word "copy"

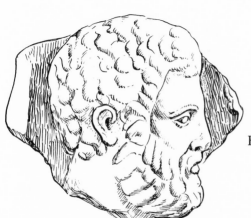

Fragments of grave reliefs, *Hamburg*

has come into ill repute in recent years, and small wonder when we consider the run-of-the-mill copies, generally multilated by overcleaning and recutting, disfigured by clumsy, arbitrary, or even outright erroneous restorations, and set up in dreary row on row, with little regard for their intrinsic worth or interest, in such venerable institutions as the Louvre, the Museo Nazionale, Naples, or the British Museum. But without them our knowledge of Greek sculpture would be as fragmentary as our knowledge of Greek poetry, drama, or philosophy without medieval manuscripts.

Let us, therefore, consider the Roman copies afresh as works of art. We must begin by removing the unsightly restorations added like lifeless prosthetics by generations that valued completeness above all else. Where we cannot discard the restorations in fact, let us attempt to do so in our mind's eye. Let us isolate the precious core, be it a torso or a head. The extremities—arms, noses, legs, and the member formerly covered by a fig leaf—are of course the most susceptible to damage, and these parts must be subjected to close scrutiny. Modern art criticism has taught us to value the honest fragment, and this concept is making itself felt in museums the world over, where marble restorations are being dismantled and banished to the storerooms and where plaster noses and penises are removed. (cf. p. 40.)

What Is a Roman Copy?

The era of the copyist began late in the second century B.C. Rome had recently become the wealthiest nation in the world at the expense of her tired, if older and more sophisticated, neighbors. Basking in affluence, she had spawned a class of art collectors and connoisseurs. These men included the most powerful and influential figures in Roman public life, such as Cicero and Varro, and later the Roman emperors.

For the Romans, "collecting" meant collecting Greek art. Greece was at this time the arbiter of taste and refinement; there were few Roman artists.

As the collecting fashion spread and the supply of Greek originals dwindled, some enterprising individuals—probably Greeks—began producing free-hand replicas to satisfy the demand. These were the first Roman copies. They consisted largely of *opera nobilia,* or works by the great sculptors—the national treasures of their day.

In about the year 100 B.C. the pointing machine was invented, and mass production began. This ingenious device, still employed by copyists the world over in essentially its ancient form, consists of vertical and horizontal sliding armatures capable of transferring points from a plaster cast taken of the original to the block of stone being worked. Using the points to guide his hand, even a relatively untalented artist could turn out an exact likeness of the Greek original before him. He could enlarge or reduce the original at will simply by changing the ratio of his armatures. He could, moreover, make copies of copies, a fact that accounts for the great number of replicas that have survived.

How Do Roman Copies Differ from Greek Originals?

This question is a complex one to answer. Much depends on the nature, date, and, above all, the quality of the copy. By and large it may be said that the difference between the original and the copy lies skin deep. That is to say, it consists mainly of the surface—the outermost skin, or "epidermis"—of the marble. It is by the quality of the final finish that copies divide into excellent, good, fair, or outright dull. For here, in the last stage of the copying process, the pointing machine was no longer of any avail, and the copyist was forced to put his talent as a sculptor to the test. A fine Roman copy can hardly be distinguished from a Greek original, as any expert on the subject will agree. Gisela M. A. Richter once offered the following advice: "To learn to know the difference between originals and copies, study originals, originals, and more originals!" While endorsing this excellent adage wholeheartedly, I would add a few practical rules of thumb. A handy criterion to the question "original" or "copy" is the nature of the marble: study the stone carefully. A Greek original must be of Greek marble, for the Greeks had such excellent quarries of their own that there was no need for them to import marble from abroad. The commonest variety is known as "Pentelic," after Mount Pentelikon near Athens, where it is quarried. It is distinguished by its warm milky color and fine grain. If it has lain for many centuries in the Attic soil, its surface takes on a golden-ruddy complexion, rather like doeskin. Also favored by the Greeks were the fine island quarries of Naxos and Paros. The former produced a gleaming white marble of large crystalline structure, similar in appearance to cube sugar; the latter is somewhat finer grained and more transparent.

"Pentelic" and "island" marbles differ markedly from the marbles most frequently employed by Roman copyists and obtained by them from the great Italian quarries of Luna and Carrara near Pisa (also employed by Michelangelo for his "David," and still exploited today). This Italian marble is opaque and extremely fine-grained; it often contains bluish-gray veins.

Important point: The Italian quarries were not worked before the middle of the first century B.C.

Mention must be made of the many colored stones and marbles found in classical sculptures. They are all Roman. Green schist, purple porphyry, black basalt, orange *giallo antico*—these appealed to the Roman taste for splendor (and were probably abhorred by the conservative Greeks). Beware of small works in hard and semi-precious stone (rock crystal, serpentine, agate, and so on); their antiquity is extremely difficult to ascertain. Such works were popular also during the Italian Renaissance. They were produced with great virtuosity in the seventeenth and eighteenth centuries and, again, in the twentieth, by the firm of Augusto Valenzi in Rome. A note of qualification: While it can be axiomatically stated that a sculpture in white North Italian or exotic colored marble can never be a Greek original, the converse does not hold true. Indeed, the best Roman copies are those carved of Pentelic and other Greek marbles—made in Greece by Greeks catering to the Roman trade.

Fortunately, good Roman copies exist to make up, in part, for the loss of originals by the great sculptors of the Classical Age. They permit us to appreciate the style and the technique of the lost originals, and thereby to admire the genius of Greek sculpture. A good Roman copy is in many ways preferable to a poor original.

The Great Sculptors of the Classical Period

Myron, active in the third quarter of the fifth century B.C., is best known for his "Discobolus," or "Discus Thrower," which survives in several Roman copies. In this work, the static instant between the windup and the throw is shown. The athlete has dug his toes into the ground, filled his lungs with air, and is about to unwind in a powerful fling. The spiral composition is a brilliant one, the work as fine a study in arrested motion as ever attempted.

The Myronian "Herakles" has survived in two replicas only, the exquisite marble statuette in the Museum of Fine Arts, Boston (Fig. 18), and a similar piece in the Ashmolean Museum, Oxford. The hero's face preserves certain vestiges of the Archaic style, especially in the treatment of his beard and curly hair, but the stylistic kinship with the "Discus Thrower" is apparent. The standing "Herakles" is a perfect example of an excellent small-scale replica of an *opus nobile* produced with the aid of a pointing machine. The sculpture is a gem of precision carving, undoubtedly made to the order of a discerning Roman collector.

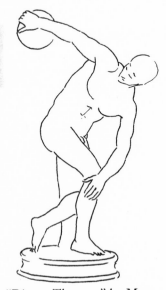

"Discus Thrower" by Myron

Fig. 18. Statuette of Herakles. Roman reduced marble copy of a bronze statue by Myron. Courtesy, Museum of Fine Arts, Boston. Acc. no. 14.733.
Museum photograph.

Myronian "Athena," *Frankfurt*

The Greek *opera nobili,* or great works, were generally cast in bronze. Roman copyists, however, worked mainly in marble. The presence of a tree trunk, strut, or other support in a marble sculpture is a sure indication that the work is a copy. The bronze original would have stood without such assistance.

Peripatetic Pausanias, the Fielding of his day, saw the original of Myron's famed "Athena and Marsyas" group when it still stood *in situ* on the Acropolis of Athens. According to legend, the goddess Athena had invented the flute, only to cast it aside on discovering that it distorted her facial features. The satyr Marsyas, concealed nearby, snatched up the discarded instrument and soon became so skillful at playing it that he decided to challenge Apollo, the god of music, to a contest. Marsyas lost, of course, and was flayed alive in punishment for his overbearing pride, or *hybris,* one of the Greek cardinal sins. The first part of this moral tale is illustrated by the Myronian composition, the Athena-half of which has survived in a number of fine copies (the Marsyas in only one). The best-known Myronian "Athena" is in the municipal museum of Frankfurt. In this work, Athena is seen as a young girl. The torso, with its simple lines and fall of drapery, is eloquently expressive of virginal divinity. A lovely Myronian head of Athena—without the body—is in Dresden (Fig. 19).

Like Myron, who was his contemporary, **Phidias** embellished the Athenian Acropolis with sculptures. He worked in gold and ivory as well as in bronze and marble, and his famous cult images of Zeus and Athena, made for the temples at Olympia and Athens respectively, were huge "chryselephantine" productions, that is, they were made of gold and ivory and fitted over a wooden core. Small-scale "souvenir" copies of both works, as well as reflections in other media (especially coins) survive to this day. The Phidian "Athena Lemnia" shows the warrior goddess at rest. The figure was set up on the Athenian Acropolis by the people of Lemnos in 445 B.C. It too has come down to us in a number of copies and adaptations.

Fig. 19. Head of Athena. From a Roman copy of a bronze statue by Myron. Dresden, Albertinum.
Museum photograph.

Perhaps the most beautiful Phidian work known to us in Roman copies is the so-called "Kassel Apollo," named after a replica in the Staatliche Kunstsammlungen of Kassel, Germany (Fig. 20). The god stands naked, holding his bow and another attribute, probably a twig of laurel. His countenance is serene, as befitting the god of music, light, and reason; his easy stance conveys an air of immense assurance and superiority. The artfully arranged locks that frame the countenance and fall in graceful corkscrew spirals to the shoulders are carefully engraved. Their scrolls, in fact, have hollowed centers—an indication that the original was cast in bronze. Note, too, the support in the form of a tree trunk (against which the god's quiver has been placed), the typical copyist's addition.

While the "Kassel Apollo" is impressive as a virtually intact ancient marble, its surface has suffered from overcleaning and recutting. This is not the case with the Karlsruhe head (Fig. 21), an "unspoiled" replica of the same original. Notice the difference in the handling of the long corkscrew lock to the left of the god's head. Whereas the copyist of the "Kassel Apollo" has taken pains to convey the effect of a metal scroll, the copyist of the Karlsruhe head has translated the metal curls into terms of marble sculpture. Such variations between several replicas of one original are not uncommon. A collector contemplating the acquisition of a Roman copy must, therefore, compare the piece in question to all other known replicas of the type. Only by so doing can he determine both the quality of the copy and the degree of fidelity to the Greek original.

Works in the Phidian style exist in a number of private collections, one of the finest examples in the United States being the head of a youth, in the possession of Professor Watkins of New Haven, Connecticut (Fig. 22). Some scholars see a fifth-century original in this small masterpiece; others have claimed it to be a Roman copy.

The last great master of the second half of the fifth century was **Polyclitus of Argos.** Like Myron, he worked primarily in bronze. His "Doryphoros," or "Spear Bearer," was famous in antiquity for its carefully studied and harmonious proportions. The work was intended to serve as a canon of perfection, and was regarded as such by generations of sculptors. A youthful athlete is shown moving forward at an easy trot, carrying a spear over one shoulder. His head is turned slightly to one side. His weight seems to be supported entirely by one leg, and the pronounced movement of his hips is beautifully interpreted in the muscular rhythm of the entire torso.

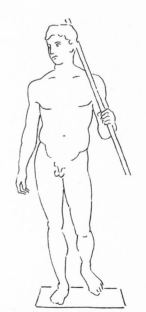

"Spear Bearer" by Polyclitus

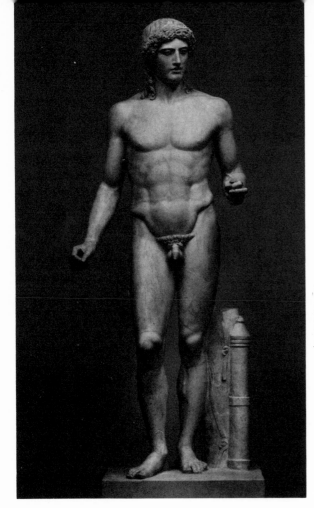

Fig. 20. The "Kassel Apollo." Roman copy of a Greek bronze believed to be the work of Phidias. Staatliche Kunstsammlungen, Kassel. Bieber, no. 1.
Museum photograph.

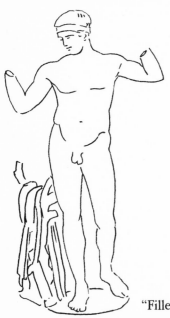

"Fillet Binder" by Polyclitus

The second famous work of Polyclitus, also immensely celebrated throughout antiquity and hence widely copied in Roman times, is the "Diadoumenos," or "Fillet Binder." A youthful victor is represented frontally, tying a sash around his head. His bodily proportions are the same as those of the "Doryphoros," and there is also the same emphasis on the musculature of the groin, suggestive of long training and intensive bodily development, that characterizes the other work. As in the case of the "Kassel Apollo," a lateral support, disturbing to the harmony of the composition, informs us that the Greek original must have been cast in bronze.

Although the "Doryphoros" and the "Diadoumenos" are the most famous Polyclitan works to have survived in copies, a great many others, either by the master himself or by his pupils, are associated with Polyclitus of Argos in style.

Fig. 21. Head of Apollo. Roman copy of the "Kassel Apollo" type. Badisches Landesmuseum, Karlsruhe. Inv. no. 59/40. *Museum photograph.*

Fig. 22. Head of a youth, from a relief. Attic. Later 5th century B.C. ("Parthenon style"). Collection of Professor Frederick M. Watkins, New Haven.
Photograph: courtesy of Fogg Art Museum, Harvard University.

The term "Polyclitan" is, in fact, today generally employed to mean "in the style of Polyclitus." In this sense the fine male torso in the Joseph Ternbach collection, New York (Figs. 23a, 23b), can be described as "Polyclitan."

The Athenian sculptor **Praxiteles** was born around 400 B.C. His career seems to have extended into the 330's or even later. Owing to his influence, the Polyclitan "canon," which stressed the rational interrelationship of bodily parts, was abandoned toward the middle of the fourth century B.C. in favor of the new "Praxitelean" style, which was essentially anti-rational, soft, and diffused—*sfumato* in the language of Italian painting. Praxiteles' masterpieces usually show youthful gods and goddesses in beautiful languid poses. Ancient authors praised Praxiteles for "putting a soul into stone"; one might also consider his works the first sexual interpretations of Greek divinity.

The "Aphrodite" that Praxiteles carved in marble for the city of Knidos in Asia Minor excels in soulful sensuality. The goddess is represented nude, in itself a revolutionary concept. One hand partly covers her breasts; the other is coyly placed over her sex. Other Praxitelean Venuses show the goddess draped to the hips, for example, the famous "Venus de Milo." Innumerable Roman copies of Praxitelean Aphrodites exist, in every size, in various materials, and of every degree of quality. They were obviously very popular with Roman collectors—and with our grandfathers as well. No Victorian smoking room was complete without one (be it only a modern imitation). It is therefore not astonishing that the Metropolitan Museum possesses nearly a dozen ancient examples, nearly all late-nineteenth-century donations (Figs. 24, 25).

Other works by Praxiteles frequently encountered in Roman copies are

"Aphrodite" by Praxiteles

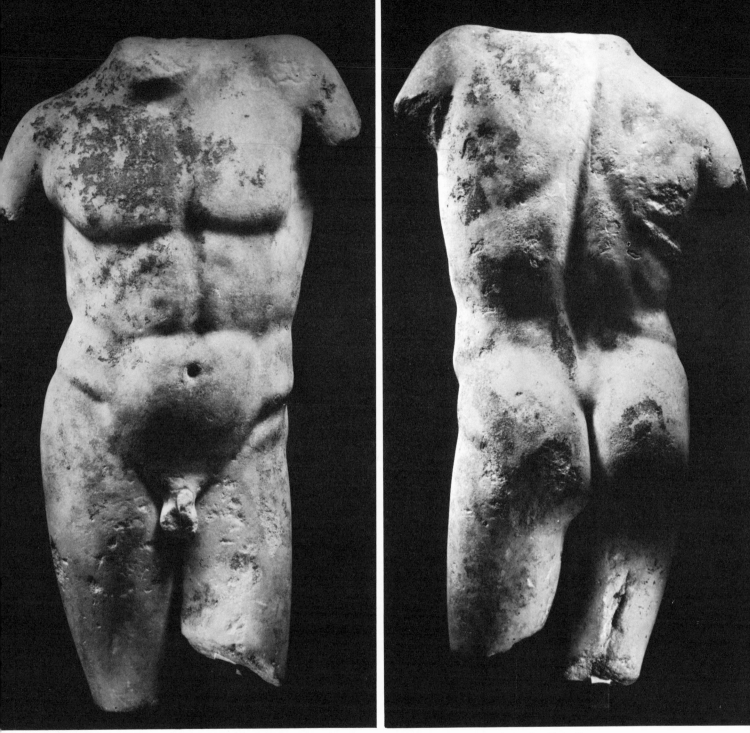

Figs. 23a, 23b. Male torso. Roman copy of a Greek original in the Polyclitan style. Collection of Joseph Ternbach, Great Neck, New York.
Photograph: courtesy of the owner.

the "Apollo," the "Hermes," and the "Satyr." The three resemble one another, both in style and spirit, each representing an effete youth in a graceful leaning pose.

With perseverance any collector of moderate means can still acquire a good Roman copy of a work by one of the greatest artistic talents produced by ancient Greece. In a few years this may no longer be true. A head of Athena (indentifiable by the traces of a helmet in back), which exhibits all the characteristics of the Praxitelean style—the dreamy eyes, the sensitively modeled mouth, the impressionistic hair—recently entered a New York private collection (Figs. 26a, 26b).

Scopas of Argos, the most famous rival of Praxiteles, and with whom he occasionally collaborated on commissions, is one of the few Greek sculptors of the Classical Age whose style is known to us in originals as well as copies. The pedimental sculptures from the reconstructed Temple of Athena at Tegea (the old temple burned down in 394 B.C.) were executed by his hand or under his direction. The fragments that have come down to us include the heads of two heroes and the much damaged head of a boar. Related in style to these Tegea sculptures are a "Herakles" (the best Roman copy of which was acquired a few years ago by Paul Getty from the renowned Lansdowne House collection) and a "Meleager" (the finest copy of which can be found in the Fogg Museum of Harvard University [Fig. 27]). The key aspects of these works are pathos (eyes turned up and set under heavy brows that cast suggestive shadows, lips parted) and impressionism (unruly hair vaguely suggested as a shaggy mass), two trends in ancient sculpture that clearly foreshadow the art of the Hellenistic Age. *(See also* Fig. 28.)

These elements may be detected in numerous other works, both originals and copies, and the term "Scopasian," like "Polyclitan," "Phidian," and "Praxi-

Fig. 24. Statuette torso of Aphrodite Anadyomene. Smaller Roman copy of a Greek original by Praxiteles. Courtesy of the Trustees, Metropolitan Museum of Art, New York. Acc. no. 27.122.17. Fletcher Fund, 1927.
Museum photograph.

Fig. 25. Statuette of Aphrodite Anadyomene. Smaller Roman copy of a Greek original by Praxiteles. Courtesy of the Trustees, Metropolitan Museum of Art, New York. Acc. no. 50.10. Gift of John W. Cross, 1950.
Museum photograph.

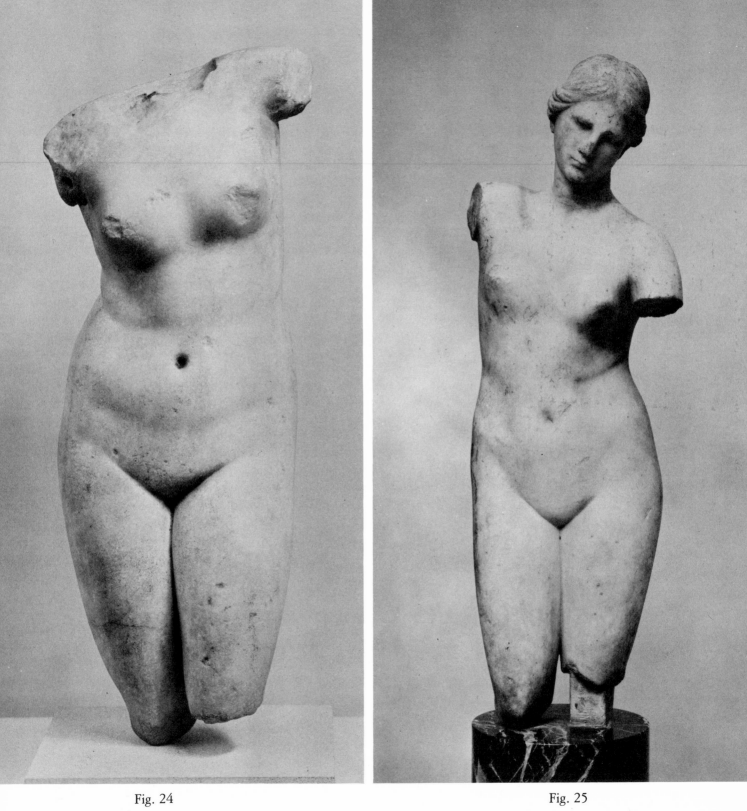

Fig. 24   Fig. 25

Figs. 26a, 26b. Head of Athena. Third century B.C. Private collection, New York.
Photograph: courtesy of the owner.

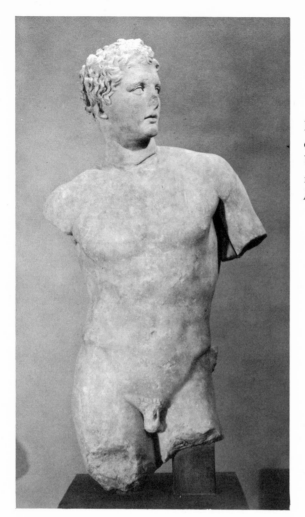

Fig. 27. Statue of Meleager. Roman copy of a Greek original by Scopas. Fogg Art Museum, Harvard University. Acc. no. 1926.48. Bequest, Mrs. Kenneth G. T. Webster.
Museum photograph.

Fig. 28. Head of Meleager. Roman copy of the "Fogg Meleager" type. Fogg Art Museum, Harvard University. Acc. no. 1913.28. Purchase from the Van Rensselaer Fund.
Museum photograph.

telean," has come to signify the style of dynamism and pathos that underlies virtually all Greek relief sculpture, and much of the sculpture in the round, dating from the second half of the fourth century B.C.

Like Myron and Polyclitus before him (but unlike Phidias, Praxiteles, and Scopas), **Lysippus of Sicyon** worked chiefly in bronze. He is best known as the court artist of Alexander the Great (356-323 B.C.). Together with Myron, Lysippus can be considered as one of the precursors of the Hellenistic style. His "Apoxymenos," a naked youth scraping his arm with a strigil, displays elegant and slender proportions. Characteristically "Lysippan" is the youth's markedly small head in relation to his elongated body. The vague and unfocused gaze of the eyes are a feature of latter-fourth-century art encountered earlier in our discussion of grave reliefs (cf. p. 11).

Like the "Venus" of Praxiteles, the Lysippan "Eros" must have been close to the hearts of the Romans, judging by the number of copies that have been found. The young love god is represented in the act of stringing his bow. This work has been called the first real child in Greek art. The charmingly youthful torso with its marvelous contrasts of direction is at once recognizable as Lysippan, even in replicas where the head, arms, and legs are not preserved. Also of interest is the Lysippan "Herakles," the forerunner of the Hellenistic muscle-bound heroes, and a masterful study of a tired strong man sitting down to rest. We recognize virtually the same facial features in most Lysippan works, including the portraits of Alexander.

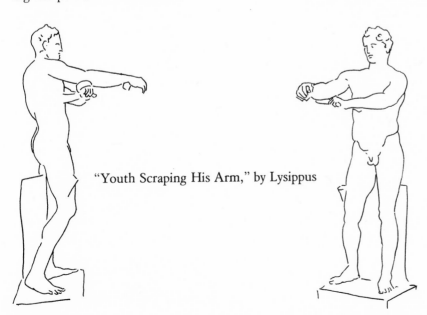

"Youth Scraping His Arm," by Lysippus

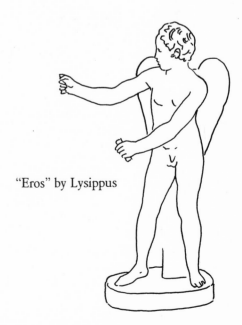

"Eros" by Lysippus

Fig. 29. Portrait of Homer. Hellenistic
period. Courtesy of the Museum of
Fine Arts, Boston. Acc. no. 04.13.
Pierce Fund.
Museum photograph.

Greek Portraits

Whereas most Greek masterworks that have come down to us in Roman copies are torsos without heads, a good number of heads without torsos have also survived by way of compensation. Of these, Greek portraits are a most interesting subject for the private collector. In these works we are brought face to face with some of the greatest personalities in the history of the Western world.

Although the ancient Egyptians had achieved realism in portraiture as early as 2500 B.C., it remained for the Greeks to penetrate deeply into the psychology of their subjects. Greek portraits include most of the prominent men of Greek antiquity: poets, orators, generals, philosophers, and statesmen. Some are contemporary (and therefore presumably faithful) likenesses; others are obviously idealized. Pliny, in describing the portrait of the ruler Pericles set up on the Athenian Acropolis, writes, "It is marvelous that in this art noble men were made to appear still nobler."

Imaginary portraits invented years or even centuries after the lifetime of the person represented are also known. They are, in fact, often the basis of Renaissance portraits of famous Greeks that, in turn, determine our own conception of their appearance. Thus, for example, several versions exist of a portrait of Homer (who probably lived in the eighth century B.C.) which was certainly "invented." They agree on only one detail: the poet's blindness. The Hellenistic interpretation of Homer, showing the venerable old man with shaggy locks, furrowed brows, and "inspired" sightless gaze directed upward, was apparently the type most admired by the Romans, for more replicas of this version exist than of all other types combined. In the finest of the extant copies (Fig. 29), which is in Boston, the poet's sightlessness is graphically suggested by the partial lowering of the upper lid. It is a replica of this Homer that appears in Rembrandt's celebrated "Aristotle Contemplating a Bust of Homer," recently purchased by the Metropolitan Museum of Art.

In the following pages we shall take up some of the more interesting Greek portraits that exist in a fair number of Roman copies and that might, therefore, appear on the antiquities market.

Socrates, perhaps the best-known and most beloved Greek philosopher, lived from 469 to 399 B.C. Portraits, two of which are inscribed with his name, show him like the Silenus whom Plato says that he resembled: bald head, domed brow, bulbous nose, thick lips—a rather unattractive assortment of physiognomical characteristics. Yet the portraits, despite the blatant ugliness of the individual traits, convey an impression of remarkable character.

Plato is also known to us in a series of portraits. Of these, an example in

Portrait of Socrates,
Museum of Fine Arts, Boston

"Portrait of Aristotle,"
Museo Nazionale, Rome

a Geneva private collection (Figs. 30a, 30b) probably stands closest to the Greek original. The subject has a broad and powerful forehead, a fine, aristocratic nose, and a carefully groomed beard, creating the impression of a distinguished man of the world. Most of the preserved Plato replicas are derived by the "pointing" process from a single master portrait. The personality represented is obviously a thinker of imposing intellect.

Euripides, by contrast, emerges in his portraits as a withdrawn and uncongenial artist, an impression of his character confirmed by the biographer Suidas, who calls him "morose, unsmiling and unsociable . . . a hater of women."

Eighteen portraits of **Aristotle** exist, and many fine heads of Stoic and Epicurean philosophers have also come down to us. **Chrysippus** and **Epicurus** are best studied in two likenesses in the Metropolitan Museum of Art.

Figs. 30a, 30b. Portrait of Plato. Roman copy of a Greek original of the 4th century B.C. Private collection, Geneva.
Photograph: H. Bloesch.

The most frequently portrayed Greek, however, was undoubtedly **Menander** (ca. 342-293 B.C.), the founder of the popular "New Comedy." Over fifty marble portraits of him have come down to us in copies—more than of any other Greek celebrity—and they all appear to go back to a single statue that was set up in the poet's honor during his lifetime in the theatre of Athens (the base, inscribed with his name, has actually been found). The portrait of Menander (Figs. 31a, 31b) shows the poet as he is described by Suidas "cross-eyed but of nimble mind." It is the portrait of a leanly handsome and intelligent man in early middle age. His lips are parted as if about to speak. His forehead is wrinkled in a preoccupied frown, and the down-turned mouth contributes to a somewhat dour expression. This is certainly one of the most arresting of all Greek portraits.

Figs. 31a, 31b. Portrait of the poet Menander. Roman copy of a Greek original of the early Hellenistic period. Museum für Kunst und Gewerbe, Hamburg. Inv. no. 1964,327. *Museum photograph.*

The last portrait to be considered is that of **Alexander the Great.** Alexander remained a popular hero throughout antiquity, and portraits of him were carved as late as the fourth century A.D. In addition to the many Roman copies, a small number of Greek originals have also come down to us. The finest, showing Alexander wearing a lion skin, is in the Boston Museum of Fine Arts (Fig. 32). The head, possibly broken from a relief, shows the youngish ruler in the

Fig. 32. Head of Alexander the Great as Herakles, from a relief. Believed to be a Greek original carved perhaps during the lifetime of the ruler (356 - 323 B.C.). Courtesy of the Museum of Fine Arts, Boston. Acc. no. 52.1741. *Museum photograph.*

semimythical guise of "New Herakles" which he fancied for himself. A small alabaster bust of Alexander in the Brooklyn Museum (Fig. 33) shows the ruler's hair arranged in the manner of a lion's mane, the Alexander coiffure made canonical by Lysippus, Alexander's official portraitist. The Brooklyn bust, which is of later Hellenistic date, was apparently once set into a statuette, perhaps of a contrasting material.

Fig. 33. Alabaster bust of Alexander the Great. From Egypt. Hellenistic, 2nd century B.C. Brooklyn Museum. Acc. no. 54.162. Charles Edwin Wilbour Fund. *Museum photograph.*

WHAT TO LOOK FOR IN MARBLE SCULPTURE

Here, finally, are a few practical tips for the collector contemplating the purchase of an ancient marble sculpture. As with any work of art, look carefully for restorations and reworked surfaces. The former are not always easy to identify, especially when they are of the same type of marble as the ancient parts and have been exposed to the elements for decades or even centuries. Joining cut edges (rather than joining breaks) should be a cause for suspicion, for it is virtually impossible to produce a modern restoration such as an arm or a nose that will fit a break exactly. The broken surface to which the restoration is to be fitted is usually prepared by sawing or filing. Sometimes an approximate joint is produced, and the gaps are smeared with plaster.

Two pieces of marble quarried at different times are rarely identical in color and crystalline structure. A modern restoration can therefore often be detected simply by a close observation of the stone. A hand lens—preferably of tenfold or stronger magnification—will be found to be an indispensable aid. Examine fresh breaks (rather than weathered or discolored surfaces), and note the color and grain of the marble closely. Is the material of all parts the same?

Watch also for recut, scraped, or otherwise maltreated surfaces. Look especially at the eyes and mouth. Damages to these two vital areas are often concealed by smearing or recutting.

The surface of a marble may be rendered "dead" by brutal scraping or scouring to remove a stubborn incrustation. Italian art dealers especially still engage in this barbaric practice. When the surface of an ancient marble looks slippery or wet, the chances are that it has been cleaned with acid—a technique employed extensively during the nineteenth century.

If a statue is very much restored, the question is whether the original "core" that remains after the restorations have been removed is worth acquiring—and if so, at what price.

Having acquired a restored piece of sculpture, we must decide whether to remove the restorations or to live with them. While this is essentially a matter of individual taste, the following two questions must be posed: Do the restorations falsify the impression of the original (as transmitted by other, better preserved, copies)? Are they aesthetically pleasing?

Not all restorations can be removed without danger of disfiguring the original. Plaster restorations present no problem: they can readily be chipped away. But marble restorations are another matter. This applies especially to noses: the trimmed flat surface that remains after the restoration is removed is unsightly. Moreover, the restored nose has often been attached with an iron dowel that must either be cut off or extracted—in both cases leaving an ugly scar. The restorer of the Copenhagen Glyptothek has devised an ingenious solution to this problem. He removes the restoration and then covers the trimmed surface of the original with an "artificial break" composed of marble filings (usually drilled from the under surface of the object) mixed with a base of colorless cement and dabbed on with the broken end of a stick. These "artificial breaks" are a happy solution to the problem, but I must confess that my own experiments with this technique were less than entirely successful.

SELECT BIBLIOGRAPHY

J. D. Beazley and B. Ashmole, *Greek Sculpture and Painting to the End of the Hellenistic Period* (Cambridge: Cambridge University Press, 1932), reprinted in 1966 with minor additions. A brief and well-written account.

M. Bieber, *The Sculpture of the Hellenistic Age* (New York: Columbia University Press, 1955).

J. Boardman, J. Dörig, W. Fuchs, M. Hirmer, *Greek Art* (Munich: Hirmir Verlag, 1966). Useful texts and over 300 superb Hirmer photographs.

R. Carpenter, *Greek Sculpture* (Chicago: University of Chicago Press, 1960).

L. Caskey, *Catalog of Greek and Roman Sculpture* (Cambridge: Harvard University Press, 1925). The Boston Museum of Fine Arts' sculpture catalog. Long out of print but can be consulted in the museum's reference library.

G. M. A. Richter, *The Sculpture and Sculptors of the Greeks* (New Haven: Yale University Press, revised edition 1950). Still a standard work on the subject in the English language. Ample bibliography.

————, *Catalog of Greek Sculptures* (New York: Metropolitan Museum of Art, 1954). A good point of departure for anyone desiring to study Greek sculpture vis-a-vis the originals. It can be consulted in the museum's reference library.

————, *The Portraits of the Greeks* (London and New York: Phaidon Press, 1965). In three volumes, with 2,100 illustrations.

Fig. 34. Hydria. Second half, 4th century B.C. On the lip, incised in punched dots, is an inscription which can be read "Charonidas, greetings" or "Charonidas, farewell" (depending on whether the hydria was inscribed as a gift or as a burial furnishing). Virginia Museum of Fine Arts, Richmond. Acc. no. 57-18. Purchase from the Williams Fund.
Museum photograph.

2

Bronzes

The miniature world of Greek bronzes has appealed to collectors for centuries. In fact, possibly more than any other art form, they can be a source of enjoyment to both collector and curator alike. The pleasure to be derived from Greek bronzes is not only visual but essentially tactile, for they must be handled to be fully appreciated.

A common notion regarding Greek bronzes is that they are priced beyond the reach of the average collector. This may be true if we think only in terms of the free-standing votive statuette; but the range of Greek bronzes available is actually far wider. It also includes the figural decorations of utilitarian objects in the widest sense of the term. These may include vessels, household implements, furnishings, tools, arms and armor, personal ornaments, mirrors, amulets, the trappings of horses, the fittings of chariots—indeed every conceivable form of object employed by the Greeks in their daily life. In ancient Greece even the meanest domestic object was generally decorated, and thereby transformed into a work of art. In this chapter, which does not pretend to be comprehensive, we can only mention a few of the many types of Greek bronzes that the collector may reasonably expect to encounter. Bronze statuettes are rare on today's market, and therefore will be dealt with last.

BRONZE VESSELS AND THEIR ATTACHMENTS

The applied ornaments of bronze vessels form a substantial part, if not indeed the majority, of all Greek bronzes to have survived. The bodies of the vessels were nearly always hammered of thin sheet metal, and have in most cases corroded away, whereas the ornaments and adjuncts were cast solid, and have survived. Larger vases, such as hydriae (water jars) and kraters (mixing bowls), often bore beautiful ornaments applied in relief (Fig. 34). In the case of the smaller bronze vases, such as oinochoes (wine pitchers) and amphorae, the plastic decoration was usually confined to the handle adjunct. These separate parts can stand alone as works of art even when divorced from their original context. Sometimes they take the form of animals; sometimes they are anthropomorphic.

Determining whether a bronze figure is an ornament of a vessel or of some other utilitarian object—or whether it was perhaps created as a free-standing statuette—can be difficult. A number of minor details will help to identify a utilitarian bronze and offer a clue to the function the object originally served. The presence of a rivet hole or a rivet in a bronze figurine is the best indication that the object was formerly attached to some background—in the majority of cases, the lid, rim, or shoulder of a vessel. The presence of a palmette above or below a figure is also a characteristic feature of the vessel bronze, for the figurative handles of a bronze vase are usually attached by palmettes.

The next step: the "interpretation" of vessel bronzes—that is to say, establishing the shape and class of a vessel to which an isolated ornament belonged—is a rewarding pursuit. (See chart of vase shapes on page 85).

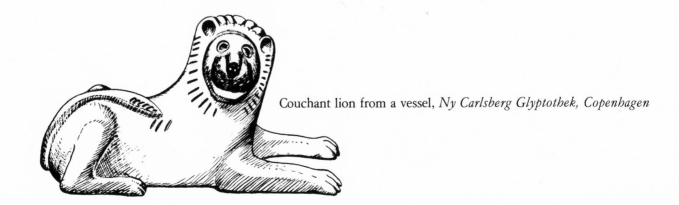

Couchant lion from a vessel, *Ny Carlsberg Glyptothek, Copenhagen*

Hydria handles, especially the vertical central handle (cf. p. 84), provided considerable scope for imaginative elaboration. Since the lateral handles and the body of the vessel were generally plain, the central handle was, in a sense, the artistic essence of the vase. Both the upper and lower terminations of the handle are frequently adorned with sculptures or reliefs, such as gorgoneia (heads of the gorgon Medusa to ward off evil) or the head of a goddess flanked by animals. One form of bronze hydria handle is topped by the head of a goddess peering over the rim of the vessel as if to protect the contents (Figs. 35a, 35b). Another form terminates at the bottom in a simple female head.

Hydria handle, *Musées Royaux, Brussels*

Vase handles, *Museum of Fine Arts, Boston*

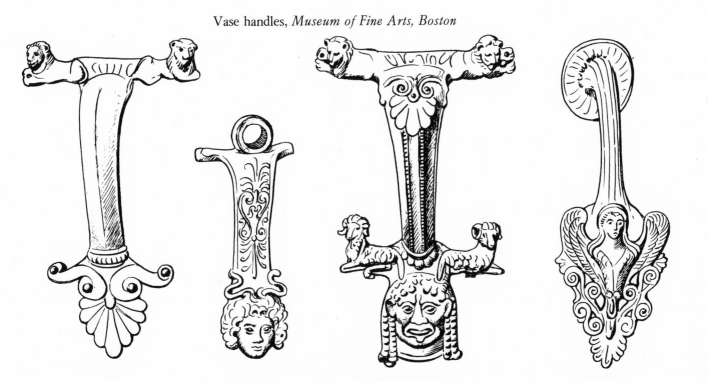

Figs. 35a, 35b. Vertical handle of a hydria.
Corinthian. Last quarter, 6th century B.C.
Courtesy of the Walters Art Gallery, Baltimore. Acc. no. 54.776.
Museum photograph.

Leaping animals sometimes turn out to be the handles of *amphorae,* although this type is rare. It seems to have been via the achemaenid East that the animoform amphora handle was introduced to Greece. A spirited leaping goat in the Metropolitan Museum of Art (Fig. 36) originally served as one handle of such an amphora. A favorite type of *oinochoe* handle, especially popular in South Italy (and also Etruria) during the Late Archaic period, takes the form of a *kouros,* or naked youth, arching backward as if performing a somersault. His hands grasp the vessel's rim; his feet rest on a palmette or ram's head that serves as the lower attachment of the handle. Sometimes these kouroi are flanked by animals — lions, rams, or both — that perch in sprightly fashion on the vessel's rim (Colorplate 2).

Paterae, or libation bowls, may also have handles in the form of naked youths, their bodies stiffly outstretched, their arms held above their heads, supporting the rim of the vessel like an architrave (Figs. 37a, 37b). There are both metropolitan Greek and South Italian versions; the latter (far more common) can generally be distinguished by the relative lack of articulation of their bodily forms.

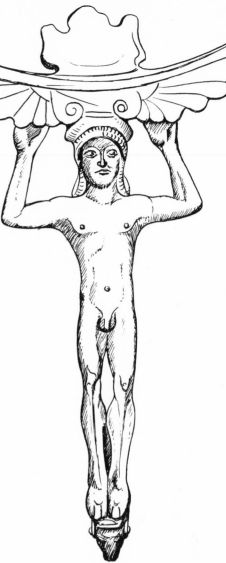

Patera handle, *Hamburg*

Fig. 36. Leaping goat. Probably the handle of an amphora. Early 5th century B.C. Courtesy of the Trustees, Metropolitan Museum of Art, New York. Acc. no. 20.181. Purchase, 1920. *Museum photograph.*

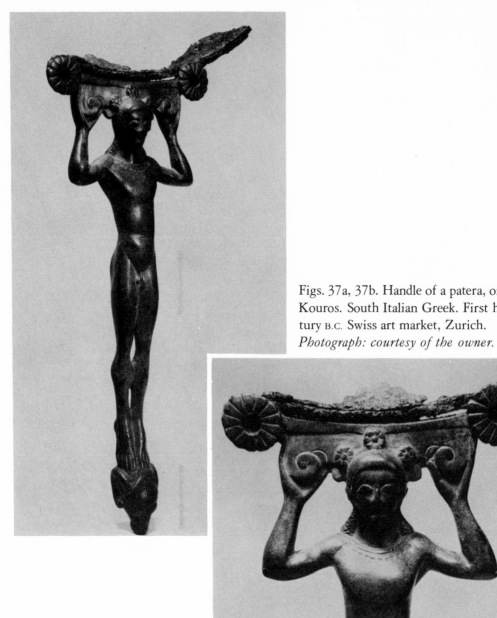

Figs. 37a, 37b. Handle of a patera, or libation bowl. Kouros. South Italian Greek. First half of 5th century B.C. Swiss art market, Zurich.
Photograph: courtesy of the owner.

Intact bronze *kraters* and *dinoi* (large mixing bowls for wine), dating from the sixth to fourth centuries B.C. have survived (Fig. 38), as have a good number of their attachments. A rampant lion with his forepaws placed on a floral scroll, in a New York private collection (Fig. 39), may be from such a vessel, as might the bronze duck heads in a number of collections (Fig. 40). Other shapes of bronze vessels, the attachments of which have come down to us, are the *lebes* (Figs. 41a, 41b), or basin, and the *situla* (Figs. 42a, 42b), a pail with swinging handle.

Running gorgon, *Metropolitan Museum of Art, New York*

Mounted archer, from a dinos, *Hamburg*

Fig. 38. Lebes (bowl or basin) with handle attachments in the form of sirens. From Vari, Attica. Middle of the 5th century B.C. Cleveland Museum of Art. Acc. no. 28.857. Gift of the John Huntington Art and Polytechnic Trust.
Museum photograph.

Opposite, above
Fig. 39. Rampant lion, perhaps from a krater. Corinthian (?). Circa 400 B.C. Formerly in the collections of the Duke of Leeds, B. W. J. Kent, Esq., A. van Branteghem, J. Hirsch, and G. Ortiz. Norbert Schimmel Collection.
Photograph: courtesy of the owner.

Opposite, below
Fig. 40. Volute handle terminating in a duck head. Fourth century B.C. Württembergisches Landesmuseum, Stuttgart. Inv. no. BAS 26.
Museum photograph.

Figs. 41a, 41b. Handle of a lebes (basin): two lions attacking a doe. From Olympia. National Museum, Athens.
Museum photograph.

Figs. 42a, 42b. Handle attachment in the form of a Herakles head, from a situla (pail). The two holes are for the swinging double handle. Late 4th century B.C. Museum of Art and Archaeology, University of Missouri, Kansas City. Acc. no. 58.2.
Museum photograph.

UTENSIL BRONZES

A vast and diverse range of unrelated objects falls under this heading: mirrors, personal ornaments, furniture decorations, arms and armor, to list just a few of them. Like vessel bronzes, utensil bronzes, too, are more often than not preserved in fragmentary condition, and divorced from their original context. The actual working parts were frequently made of iron, wood, or other perishable material, and have disappeared without a trace, so that here again the collector is confronted with the challenge of establishing the purpose for which a certain bronze decoration was created.

Mirrors

Greek mirrors are, as a class, of remarkably high quality: they are in fact the loveliest and most desirable of all utensil bronzes. The two types most frequently encountered are the standing, or "caryatid," mirror (Colorplate 3) and the box mirror, the latter generally known by the German name *Klappspiegel* (literally "folding mirror"). The finest of the standing mirrors date from the Late Archaic and Early Classical periods and have a standing figurine, generally female, as support. The mirror disk, which of course was kept highly polished in antiquity, is fastened to the top of the supporting figure's head by a flat triangular spacer often decorated at each end with a scroll. In the more elaborate examples, rosettes or little animals chasing one another are apt to be fastened to the rim. A standing mirror in the Cleveland Museum of Art may be singled out as a good illustration of the type (Figs. 43a, 43b). The mirror disk is supported by the figure of a woman clad in a simple sleeved chiton, worn belted at the waist with overfold. She stands in the traditional posture of the *kore,* or worshiper, proffering a blossom and lifting a fold of her skirt. To right and left

Mirror support, *Hamburg*

Figs. 43a, 43b. Caryatid mirror: Corinthian or Sikyonian. Circa 470-460 B.C. Cleveland Museum of Art. Acc. no. 50.7. Purchase from the J. H. Wade Fund.
Museum photograph.

Folding mirror,
Musée d'Art et d'Histoire, Geneva

of her head, fastened by rivets through the tips of their wings, hover two small winged figures. These are a standard feature of such mirrors and are generally described as "Erotes." They may, in fact, personify psychic forces such as love (Eros) and desire (Pothos).

The *Klappspiegel,* or box mirror, came into fashion as the caryatid mirror began to pass out of vogue, at the end of the fifth century B.C. It is composed of the polished mirror disk that is connected by a hinge to the mirror cover. In addition there is always a small loop for opening the mirror as well as for hanging it up when not in use. *Klappspiegel* lids are generally decorated with an applied relief worked in the repoussé technique; in some rare examples the inner surface of the lid is silver-plated and decorated with engraving. The most typical of these cover reliefs figure the head of a goddess (shown frontally, in profile, or in three-quarter view). Thetis on a hippocamp (sea horse) is shown on a mirror in Boston (Fig. 44). Many depict the goddesses and minor deities most intimately associated with cosmetics and female coquetry in general: Aphrodite, Eros, and Pan. Corinth was the most important center for the manufacture of these mirrors, but they were certainly produced elsewhere as well.

Fig. 44. Folding mirror: Thetis on a hippocamp, carrying the arms of Achilles. Greek, from Corinth. Fourth century B.C. Courtesy of the Museum of Fine Arts, Boston. Acc. no. 98.672. Pierce Fund. *Museum photograph.*

Furniture

Greek tables, chairs, beds, and other pieces of furniture were richly decorated. Generally, only the cast-bronze ornaments have survived, the wooden parts having rotted away. It is often difficult to establish exactly how a particular ornament was employed, but for one type at least there is certainty; this is the characteristic ornament of the *fulcrum,* or sloping headrest, that was fastened to one end of the *kline,* or banqueting couch. Each side of the fulcrum was fitted with a metal frame, and this was decorated at the top with the projecting head and neck of a horse, mule (Fig. 45), or other animal (Fig. 46), and at the bottom with a roundel figuring the head of Eros or of a Silen or other bacchic figure (in subtle reference to the bed's non-sleep functions). Both of these ornament types have survived in large numbers, although many date from the Roman period, when such ornaments seem to have been immensely popular. The style of the workmanship is about the only criterion for dating: in general, the Roman examples are stiffer and less lifelike than the Greek (which date mostly from the third and second centuries B.C.). Both Greek and Roman fulcrum ornaments can be very handsome, which of course explains why they have long been a favored collectors' item.

Mule's head, from a *kline, Metropolitan Museum of Art, New York*

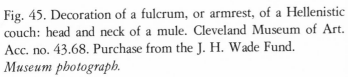

Fig. 45. Decoration of a fulcrum, or armrest, of a Hellenistic couch: head and neck of a mule. Cleveland Museum of Art. Acc. no. 43.68. Purchase from the J. H. Wade Fund. *Museum photograph.*

58

Fig. 46. Decoration of a fulcrum, or armrest, of a Hellenistic couch: elephant head. Formerly in the Durand, Pourtalès, Gréau and Loeb collections. Antikensammlungen, Munich. Sammlung Loeb. Gift of James Loeb.
Museum photograph.

Arms and Armor

The most beautiful examples of Greek arms and armor date from the Archaic and Classical periods. Whereas Greek offensive weapons are generally undecorated, their fine workmanship and harmonious proportions nevertheless make them popular with collectors. Lance heads and butts exist in many varieties. Some examples bear incised inscriptions indicating that they were dedicated in a sanctuary along with other spoils of battle. Shields were most frequently made of wood and have therefore vanished, but their ornaments remain. These include some striking blazons cut out of sheet metal and carefully incised [cocks, griffin heads, gorgoneia, serpents, and lion protomes (busts of animals) are known], as well as a series of bronze reliefs depicting mythological subjects that were fastened to the inside of the shield on either side of the arm grip. The latter have survived in some quantity, and examples continue to be found. Greek helmets can be handsome works of art even when undecorated, but the majority

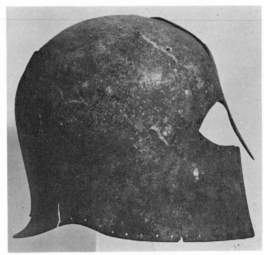

Figs. 47a, 47b. Corinthian helmet. Sixth century B.C. Museum für Kunst und Gewerbe, Hamburg. Inv. no. M832.
Photograph: Evelyn Hagenbeck.

bear some form of incised decoration, generally along the rim. Corinthian-type helmets, with their characteristic eyeholes and long nose guards, are the most sought after because of their graceful lines (Figs. 47a, 47b), and being of quite heavy construction they have withstood the centuries in large numbers. Some types of helmets dating from the Classical and Hellenistic periods have hinged cheek guards that are decorated in the repoussé technique much like the lids of *Klappspiegel* mirrors. The Berlin Museum owns a beautiful example figuring a seated Odysseus (Fig. 48). A fair number of these helmet reliefs have survived (Fig. 49).

Greek body armor (cuirasses, thigh guards, and so on) is relatively rare owing to the thinness of the metal, which makes it very susceptible to corrosion. Some fine greaves (shin guards) have entered private collections. Only recently a find of richly decorated bronze *mitrai,* or abdominal guards, from Crete, dating from the late seventh century B.C., appeared on the art market and were purchased by an American collector (Colorplate 4).

Fig. 48. Cheek guard from a helmet: seated Odysseus. From Megara. Late 5th century B.C. Staatliche Museen, Berlin (West). Inv. no. 7863.
Photograph: Jutta Tietz-Glagow.

Fig. 49. Shoulder flap from a cuirass or possibly a helmet cheekpiece: relief plaque with satyr kneeling on a rock and gazing into the distance. When purchased, the object was attached to the bronze hydria of Figure 34. Fourth century B.C. Virginia Museum of Fine Arts, Richmond. Acc. no. 57-18/A.
Museum photograph.

BRONZE STATUETTES: HISTORICAL SURVEY

Minoan Bronzes

The earliest classical bronzes (if we take the adjective in the broadest sense, as in "classical landscape") come from Minoan Crete and date from before the dawn of European history. These are small creations: the largest known example of a Minoan bronze statuette is under eight inches high. Among the types of Minoan bronzes that still occasionally find their way onto the antiquities market, male and female "worshiper" figurines are the most common. "Common" is of course used here in a relative sense: all Minoan bronzes are, in fact, quite rare and exceedingly expensive (although one wealthy collector has actually succeeded in garnering an entire vitrine full of them within the space of a few years). A representative example shows such a male worshiper standing, legs together, in a pose of rigid attention, and raising his right hand to his brow in the Cretan "salute" of adoration (Fig. 50a). The corresponding female figures generally wear flounced skirts (Figs. 50b, 50c, 50d). According to some scholars, the latter represent the Minoan nature goddess, but most are probably worshipers. Minoan bronzes were never trimmed or reworked after the casting, and their rough and unfinished appearance imbues them with spontaneous charm.

Minoan male worshiper,
Metropolitan Museum of Art, New York

Fig. 50a. Standing man (worshiper). From the Diktaean Cave, Crete. Late Minoan I, circa 1600-1500 B.C. Ashmolean Museum, Oxford. Inv. no. AE. 23. Gift of Sir Arthur Evans.
Museum photograph.

Minoan goddess or worshiper, *Museum of Fine Arts, Boston*

Figs. 50b, 50c, 50d. Standing woman (worshiper). Late Minoan I, circa 1600-1500 B.C. Staatliche Museen, Berlin (West). Inv. no. 8092.
Photograph: Jutta Tietz-Glagow.

Geometric and Orientalizing Period Bronzes

Geometric animals, *Hamburg*

A wealth of bronze statuettes has survived from the Greek Geometric period, mostly dating from the eighth century B.C. They include warriors in full armor, as well as various types of wild and domestic animals such as are also represented in the vase paintings of this period (cf. pp. 96-98). Figures in action, such as the small lyre player in Brussels (Fig. 51) and the helmetmaker in Copenhagen (Fig. 52), as well as group figures, such as the suckling fawn in Boston (Fig. 53), are relatively rare.

The most common forms of Geometric bronzes are the small votive animals that range in quality and importance from large and carefully worked pieces, such as the magnificent horse in the Metropolitan Museum of Art (Fig. 54), to primitive quadrupeds such as can be seen in many collections (Fig. 55). The latter are not without their special attractiveness, however; it is in unpretentious rustic offerings such as these that the native qualities inherent in cast and

Fig. 51. Lyre player. Cretan (?). Geometric period, 8th century B.C. Musées Royaux d'Art et d'Histoire, Brussels. Inv. no. R826.
Photograph: A.C.L.

Fig. 52. Seated helmetmaker, said to be from Olympia. Peloponnesian. Geometric, late 8th century B.C. Ny Carlsberg Glyptothek, Copenhagen. Inv. no. 3360.
Photograph: Lennert Larsen.

Fig. 53. Doe suckling fawn. Geometric period, 8th century B.C. Courtesy of the Museum of Fine Arts, Boston. Acc. no. 98.650. H. L. Pierce Fund.
Museum photograph.

Fig. 54. Horse on an openwork stand. Geometric period, second half, 8th century B.C. Courtesy of the Trustees, Metropolitan Museum of Art, New York. Acc. no. 21.88.24. Rogers Fund, 1921.
Museum photograph.

Fig. 55. Bovid. Geometric period, late 8th century B.C. Cambridge, England, Fitzwilliam Museum. Inv. no. GR 2 1933. *Photograph: Stern & Sons, Cambridge.*

Geometric bronzes, *Metropolitan Museum of Art, New York*

hammered bronze can best be appreciated. Some examples stand on a round or rectangular plinth that is perforated or worked in relief with a geometric design like that of a seal. Birds are sometimes provided with a loop for hanging; the most common are waterfowl, hens, and cocks (not "peacocks," as they are often called).

One class of Geometric bronze object is particularly widespread. This is the *fibula,* a specialty of Boeotia resembling an outsized safety pin with a large flat catchplate providing a field for engraved decoration. This decoration, frequently executed by a technique known as "tremolo"—rocking the scarper back and forth so as to produce a zigzag of arcs—generally takes the form of meanders, swastikas, and similar abstract ornaments; on the larger fibulas, ships, horses, birds, and even mythological subjects appear (Figs. 56a, 56b). *Caldrons,* or large open kettles, supported by tripods were a popular form of votive offering during the Geometric as well as the Orientalizing period of Greek art. The tripods have cast, then hammered, legs and large ring handles sometimes surmounted or straddled by figures of horses, bulls, or even human beings. Examples, both intact and fragmentary, have been found in most of the major sanctuaries of the Greek world and also in places as far afield as Anatolia (Turkey) and central France. In the Orientalizing period (seventh century B.C.), hollow-cast protomes of griffins and other monsters of Oriental inspiration were attached to the rims of the caldrons, perhaps in order to protect the contents against evil spirits (Colorplate 5). These caldron attachments include some of the most striking early Greek bronzes to have survived. A fair number, many from the famous sanctuary of Hera on the island of Samos, have found their way into museums and private collections (Fig. 57).

Caldron griffin, *Hamburg*

Figs. 56a, 56b. Engraved fibula: a lion devouring his prey on the one side; four fish on the other. Boeotian. Geometric period, 8th century B.C. D. and J. de Ménil Collection, Houston, Texas. *Photograph: courtesy of the owners.*

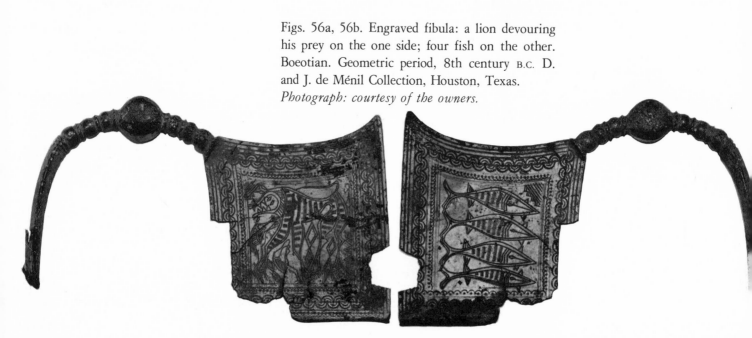

Fig. 57. Griffin protome. Late 7th century B.C. Fogg Art Museum, Harvard University. Acc. no. 1963.130. Gift of Frederick M. Watkins.
Museum photograph.

Archaic Bronzes

By the beginning of the sixth century B.C., the angular abstractionism of Geometric art, as well as the imitation of Near Eastern prototypes that characterized the art of the Orientalizing period had largely been abandoned in favor of a more naturalistic style known as the Archaic (Colorplate 6). This period has left us a great many masterpieces of bronze sculpture, many of the finest examples coming from the Peloponnese. Olympia is an important source, the Panhellenic sanctuary of Zeus at Dodona, a remote site in northern Epirus, another. This does not, however, mean that the bronzes were of necessity made in these places. Being small, these objects were easily transportable, and for that reason they were always a favorite form of votive gift to a divinity, and were carried on pilgrimages from one end of the Greek world to the other.

Individual styles of bronze working developed in various Greek centers during the Archaic period. At the very beginning, in the later seventh century B.C., the island of Crete seems to have played an important role. But by the middle of the sixth century the Cretan ateliers seem to have stopped producing. Corinth, Argos, Athens, and Sparta had developed important schools of bronze working by the beginning of the sixth century. Indeed, a fair number of regional Archaic styles can be distinguished by the amateur, with a bit of practice. Archaic and Early Classical bronze figurines made at Corinth, for example, are identifiable by their sprightly elegance, whereas the bronzes of Argos tend to be somewhat heavier and more roundish in their proportions. Athenian bronzes, especially those representing athletes, are slender and elastic, radiating intelligence and strength; they often bear a distinct family resemblance to the marble kouroi (cf. pp. 8-10). Spartan statuettes are marked by keen and pointed physiognomies, those of male figures by pronouncedly muscular anatomy, those of females by a sober, almost austere, treatment of drapery folds (Fig. 58). The comparison with bronzes of Rhodes and Samos is interesting; the latter feature markedly fleshy forms and richly elaborated draperies.

A provincial school of bronze working that deserves mention here is that of Arcadia, a remote central Peloponnesian region. While cruder to be sure than bronzes from the wealthier and more sophisticated centers, Arcadian bronze sculptures can be as delightful as any found in Greece. The choice of subject matter is somewhat limited: most often they represent animals (especially goats) or bearded shepherds with wide peasant faces who are wearing cloaks and conical felt caps (Fig. 59). An unusual example is the little ithyphallic "Warren herm"

Fig. 58. A striding Artemis (shooting her bow). Spartan. Circa 560 B.C. Staatliche Museen, Berlin (West). Inv. no. 7971.
Photograph: Jutta Tietz-Glagow.

Fig. 59. A bearded man with staff. Arcadian (?). Circa 500-480 B.C. Fogg Art Museum, Harvard University. Acc. no. 1965.533. Gift of Frederick M. Watkins.

(Figs. 60a, 60b), now in the Norbert Schimmel Collection. The tiny figure has a merry twinkle in its eye, "as if amused by his own prowess." Still another is the remarkable figure of Pan, shading his eyes, in the Berlin Museum (Figs. 61a, 61b), which, however, dates from the fifth century.

Freestanding bronze figurines from Magna Graecia are quite rare, owing, perhaps, to a local preference for vessel and utensil bronzes (see pp. 44-60) as well as terra-cottas, to serve as votive dedications. Generally speaking, the figurative bronzes of the Greek colonies of South Italy and Sicily can be said to differ from the products of the motherland by a more approximate and generalized treatment of anatomy and, in many instances, by a greater degree of spontaneity (meaning freer and more energetic poses and more unusual choice of subject matter). Collectors often tend to ignore these latter compensations and to see only the lower quality of the South Italian vis-à-vis the metropolitan Greek bronze.

Figs. 60a, 60b. Ithyphallic herm. Arcadian (?). Circa 490-480 B.C. Formerly in the collection of E. P. Warren. Norbert Schimmel Collection, New York. *Photograph: courtesy of the owner.*

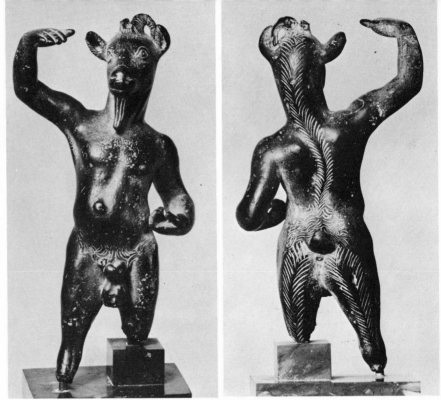

Figs. 61a, 61b. Pan shielding his eyes to peer into the distance. From Lusoi in Arcadia. Middle of the 5th century B.C. Staatliche Museen, Berlin (West). Inv. no. 8624.
Photograph: Jutta Tietz-Glagow.

Classical Bronzes

Master bronzes of the Classical period, the era from the end of the Persian Wars (479 B.C.) down to the death of Alexander (323 B.C.), are even rarer than those of the Archaic age. Production seems to have diminished radically in this period, and the scarcity of fine bronzes continues down to the Hellenistic period, when the amassing of bronze sculptures as *objets d'art* seems to have come into fashion. Regional stylistic differences are now far more difficult to recognize than before, and by 400 B.C. they have all but been replaced by a general Late Classical *koine,* or lingua franca. A few old-fashioned workshops, such as those of Arcadia and of Magna Graecia, continue on in their conservative local style.

The relatively few bronze statuettes that have survived from the Classical period are nearly all conceived under the influence of the contemporary great masters, sculptors such as Myron, Polyclitus, and Phidias (cf. pp. 20 - 33) who set the style for all Greece. The all-pervasive influence of these and other renowned artists also contributed to further negating the role of regional styles.

The small number of Classical Greek bronzes to have come down to us are nearly all of superb quality (Figs. 62, 63). We shall have to content ourselves with illustrating two typical examples: one male, the other female. The so-called *Waffenläufer* at Tübingen University, Germany (Figs. 64a, 64b), a work of about 470 B.C., depicts a helmeted but otherwise naked warrior starting in an armed footrace; he formerly carried a shield and a spear, both of which were made separately and have been lost. The free and graceful stance of the figure is a delight to the eye from any angle. The advanced knowledge of anatomy,

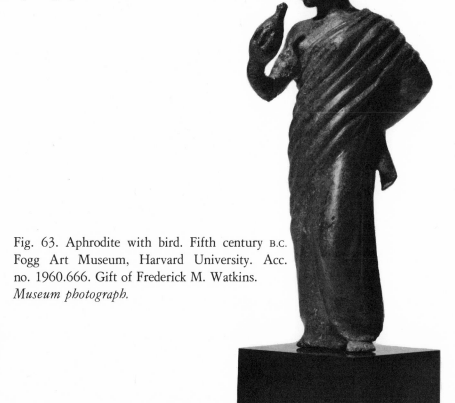

Fig. 62. The "Martussian athlete." Attic or Argive. Third quarter, 5th century B.C. Cleveland Museum of Art. Acc. no. 55.684. Gift of the Hanna Fund. *Museum photograph.*

Fig. 63. Aphrodite with bird. Fifth century B.C. Fogg Art Museum, Harvard University. Acc. no. 1960.666. Gift of Frederick M. Watkins. *Museum photograph.*

Figs. 64a, 64b. "Armed Foot Racer" *(Hoplitodromos)* leaving the starting post. He formerly carried a shield. Circa 480 B.C. Archaeological Institute of Tübingen University.
Museum photograph.

revealed by the modeling, stands in curious contrast to the neatly arranged rows of snail-like curls that line the forehead, the only vestige of Archaic style the figure reveals.

The naturalistic trends of the Late Classical period, the era of Praxiteles (cf. pp. 26, 28), find their best expression in the so-called "Maiden from Beroea" in Munich (Fig. 65). A naked girl of breathtakingly beautiful proportions, perhaps Aphrodite, perhaps a hetaera, or professional courtesan, is represented in an easy "classical" stance. This masterpiece probably dates from the beginning of the fourth century B.C., although arguments have been advanced for dating the work both in the fifth and third centuries. The piece is cast hollow, a rarity among small bronzes, which are generally cast solid; the missing arms were made separately, and doweled in.

Fig. 65. "Maiden from Beroea." Early 4th century B.C. Museum Antiker Kleinkunst, Munich. Inv. no. 3669.
Photograph: F. Kaufmann.

Hellenistic Bronzes

The establishment of new centers in the Hellenistic period brought about a considerable expansion of the bronze industry, with the result that a sizable series of fine bronzes from this period have come down to us. The majority of extant Hellenistic bronzes come from Syria and from Egypt, each of which possessed important workshops. As in the Classical period, regional styles are submerged in an international *koine* and remain extremely difficult to distinguish. The composition of the metal or the color of the patina (see pp. 80-81) tells us little, and the distinction between Syrian and Egyptian Greek bronzes of this period is most often drawn by the choice of subject matter that is represented— a criterion that is undoubtedly very often misleading. One very common Syrian type, however, is the standing figure of Aphrodite, a goddess associated in Syria with the ancient and widely venerated Astarte. Sometimes the Syrian Aphrodite is shown naked in the Classical "Praxitelean" pose; sometimes she is represented in various ritual postures of toilet, such as combing or wringing her hair, removing or putting on her sandals (Fig. 66). Examples of fine quality exist in many collections, among them the Metropolitan Museum of Art and the Museum of Fine Arts, Boston (Fig. 67). The recently dispersed de Clercq Collection of Paris, which was formed in Syria during the nineteenth cen-

Fig. 66. Aphrodite putting on or removing her sandal. Alexandrian (?). J. Paul Getty Museum, Malibu, California. Inv. no. A58.S-3. *Museum photograph.*

Fig. 67. Aphrodite (side). Hellenistic. Courtesy of the Museum of Fine Arts, Boston. Acc. no. 00.313. H. L. Pierce Collection.

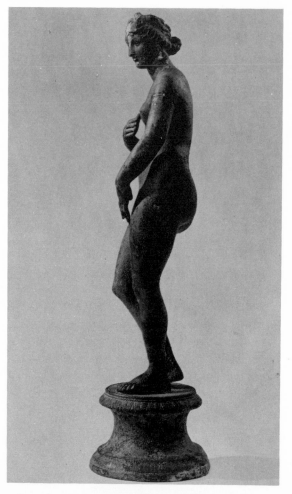

tury, contained literally dozens of excellent specimens, ranging in size from
two inches to over a foot, and many of these will undoubtedly continue to appear
on the market for some time to come.

Small "genre" figures—dancers, acrobats, musicians, and the like, represented in their characteristic occupations—are generally assigned to Alexandria (Egypt), though often without any really clinching evidence. These figures
are among the most captivating works of art the Hellenistic Age has to offer,
for they afforded sculptors an opportunity to deal with unusual subjects and
often complicated poses. The veiled dancer in the Baker Collection (Figs. 68a,
68b, 68c, 68d), a brilliant study in tangential motion, is the most distinguished
example of this category to come to mind. An unusual and dynamic pose is also
captured in the Cleveland Museum's satyr (Fig. 69), whose motion, like that
of the dancer, has been arrested with one foot off the ground.

Another favorite theme of Hellenistic bronzes, closely related to that of
"genre" figures, is the grotesque. Physical deformations and aberrations are
often portrayed with obvious relish in figurines such as dwarfs and hunchbacks.
Sometimes the representations are brutal caricatures; at other times they are
characterized by gentle pathos, as for example the figure of a young slave boy
(of Egyptian race?) squatting on a rock (Figs. 70a, 70b), a perfect portrait of
human dejection. Pygmies were a subject of special appeal to Alexandrian taste.
According to a Greek tradition going back to Homeric times, they live in Ethi-
opia and do annual battle with the migratory crane. The bronze illustrated in
our Figures 71a, 71b, was part of a group representing a pygmy and a crane:
the little fellow holds the crane by his long neck and is about to club him with
a stick. These curious statuettes, which exist in a great variety of types, are
often phallic, and it is generally supposed that they served as *porte-bonheurs,*
or lucky charms.

Arrested action also distinguishes many extraordinary animal bronzes of
this period, such as the female panther disturbed while feeding on her prey or
the wild sow brought to bay (Fig. 72). Details (like eyes, manes, or bridles) are
often inlaid in silver in the better examples.

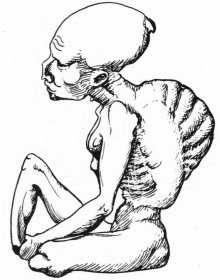

Hellenistic hunchback, *Hamburg*

Hellenistic panther, *Hamburg*

Figs. 68a, 68b, 68c, 68d. Statuette of a veiled dancer. She wears a face mask with slits for the eyes. Said to be from Alexandria. Hellenistic. Walter C. Baker Collection, New York.
Photograph: courtesy of the owner.

Fig. 69. "Piping and dancing Satyr."
Hellenistic. Third to 2nd centuries B.C.
Cleveland Museum of Art. Acc. no.
45.366. Purchase from the J. H. Wade
Fund.
Museum photograph.

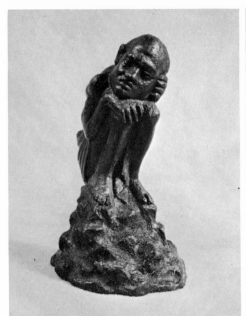

Figs. 70a, 70b. "Squatting Slave Boy." Hellenistic (Alexandrian?), 3rd - 2nd centuries B.C. Norbert Schimmel Collection, New York.
Photograph: courtesy of the owner.

Figs. 71a, 71b. "Pygmy Fighting with a Crane." Late Hellenistic (Alexandrian), 2nd - 1st centuries B.C. Norbert Schimmel Collection, New York.
Photograph: courtesy of the owner.

Fig. 72. "Sow at Bay." Greek, Hellenistic. Courtesy, Museum of Fine Arts, Boston. Acc. no. 64.510. William Francis Warden Fund.
Museum photograph.

TECHNIQUES

The principal techniques employed for working bronze in antiquity were hammering and casting. The former was used especially for vessels. Casting was generally by the *cire perdue,* or lost-wax, process, which accounts for the fact that no two Greek bronzes are alike. The smaller bronzes, including most of the ones illustrated in this chapter, were cast solid from a wax model that was encased in clay. When this clay mold was heated, the wax ran out, and the resulting negative, or envelope, was then filled with molten metal. The clay was broken to remove the bronze, which was generally carefully tooled in a cold state. Larger bronzes were cast hollow, since unequal contraction in cooling would otherwise split the metal. This was accomplished by carving a model in wood or clay and coating this with a layer of wax that was then enclosed in the terra-cotta "envelope." Sometimes the wax was applied inside the mold taken from the original. Both solid and hollow bronzes were often cast in several sections that were then assembled by doweling or with solder.

PATINA

There can be no question but that a fine patina is an asset to an ancient bronze and an important factor in determining its value. Only in rare instances, however, does a freshly excavated bronze exhibit the beautiful patina we are familiar with from looking at ancient bronzes in museums. The prized glossy green or bluish *Edelpatina* layer is generally covered by a thick outer crust of oxidation that is not only unsightly but can hide engraved and even inlaid detail. This must be carefully stripped away by a skilled technician before the beautiful under-skin becomes visible. In other words, nearly all finely patinated bronzes acquired on the market or seen on museum shelves have at one time or other passed through a restorer's hands.

Patinas vary greatly in color and texture, depending on the metallurgical composition of the bronze, the conditions to which the object has been exposed over the centuries, and—last but not least—the technique by which the object has been cleaned. While it is true that an expert can recognize the provenance of some bronzes (Olympia, South Italy, Turkey, Egypt, and so on) simply by the nature of their patina, familiarity with ancient bronzes also brings with it the in-stant recognition of certain restorers' "handwriting." Until late in the nineteenth century it was fairly common practice to "clean" bronzes by stripping them of their surface with acid or ammonia, and there are still professional restorers who resort to the no less barbaric practice of indiscriminate electrolysis. These are extremes of irresponsibility, however; far more common are bronzes that have been deliberately overcleaned in parts, creating a coloristic effect of reds, blues, and greens—the various layers of the bronze's "skin" being artfully juxta-posed one against another. Artificial patination, which the collector of bronzes must watch for with an eagle eye, will be discussed in our chapter on forgeries (although, sometimes, perfectly genuine bronzes are artificially patinated when they have been clumsily overcleaned).

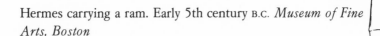

Hermes carrying a ram. Early 5th century B.C. *Museum of Fine Arts, Boston*

Athena as war goddess. First half, 5th century B.C. *Athens National Museum*

SELECT BIBLIOGRAPHY

J. Charbonneaux, *Greek Bronzes* (New York: Viking Press, 1958). Translated from the French. A perceptive summary, with many good illustrations and extensive bibliography. Good discussion of regional styles.

W. Lamb, *Greek and Roman Bronzes* (London, 1929). Still the most comprehensive general survey of the subject. A recent photomechanical reprinting differs from the original edition only by the addition of a foreword and an up-to-date bibliography by L. K. Congdon.

D. Mitten and S. F. Doeringer, *Master Bronzes from the Classical World* (Cambridge: Fogg Art Museum, 1967). Useful catalog of a loan exhibition recently held at Harvard University.

G. M. A. Richter, *Greek Bronzes* (New York: Metropolitan Museum, 1915). The best *catalogue raisonné* in English of an important and representative collection of classical bronzes. Invaluable as a reference work. Out of print but can be consulted in the museum's reference library and elsewhere.

H. B. Walters, *Catalogue of Bronzes, British Museum* (London, 1899). Useful for reference. Out of print.

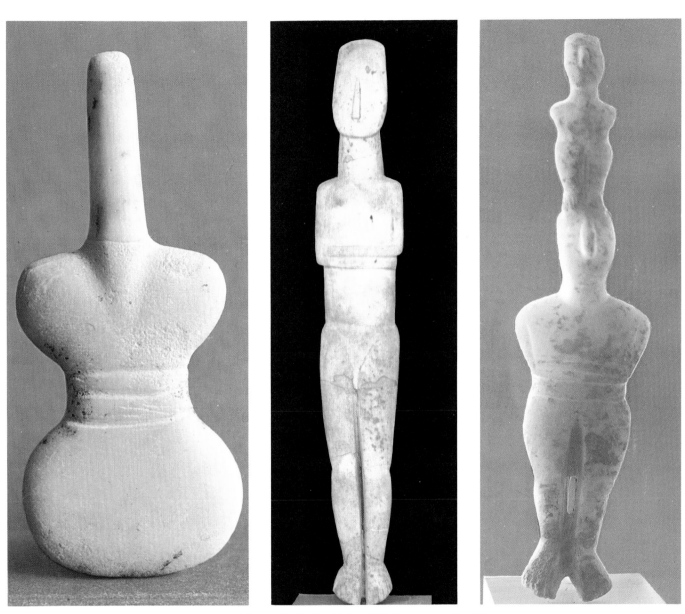

Colorplate 1. Three Cycladic idols. Third to second millennium B.C.
Badisches Landesmuseum, Karlsruhe. *Museum photographs.*

Colorplate 2. Oinochoe (wine pitcher) with anthropomorphic handle. Western Greek (Tarentine?). Circa 530–520 B.C. Leon Pomerance Collection, New York. *Photograph: courtesy of the owner.*

Colorplate 3. Caryatid mirror. Argive or Corinthian. Circa 470 B.C. Royal Ontario Museum, Toronto. Acc. no. 956.156. *Museum photograph.*

Colorplate 4. Mitra, or semicircular abdominal shield. Designed to be suspended from a belt. Two facing horse protomas are figured in relief. Inscribed "Synenitos, the son of Euklotas, took this " (as his share of the spoils of battle). Cretan. Early Archaic, late 7th century B.C. Norbert Schimmel Collection, New York. *Photograph: courtesy of the owner.*

Colorplate 5. Three griffin protomas from a caldron. Said to have been found in Gordion, Anatolia. Eastern Greek. Seventh century B.C. Private collection. *Photograph: Taylor & Dull, Inc., New York.*

Colorplate 7. Stemmed kylix from Kalymnos decorated with a stylized cuttlefish. Late Mycenaean, circa 1300–1200 B.C. Courtesy of the Trustees, British Museum, London. Inv. no. A1008. *Photograph: Peter Clayton.*

Colorplate 8. Bowl painted with a bull and a bird, from Enkomi, Cyprus. Late Mycenaean, circa 1300–1200 B.C. Courtesy of the Trustees, British Museum, London. Inv. no. C416. *Photograph: R. A. Higgins.*

Colorplate 6. The "Mantikles Apollo." Statuette of Apollo dedicated by Mantikles. The inscription on the figure's thigh reads "Mantikles dedicated [this] from his tithe to the Far Darter of the Silver Bow; do thou, Phoebus, grant gracious recompense." Seventh century B.C. Courtesy of the Museum of Fine Arts, Boston. Acc. no. 03.997. Francis Bartlett Collection. *Museum photograph.*

Colorplate 9. Attic red-figure psykter (wine cooler): dolphin riders. Attributed to Oltos. Circa 520–510 B.C. Norbert Schimmel Collection, New York. *Photograph: courtesy of the owner.*

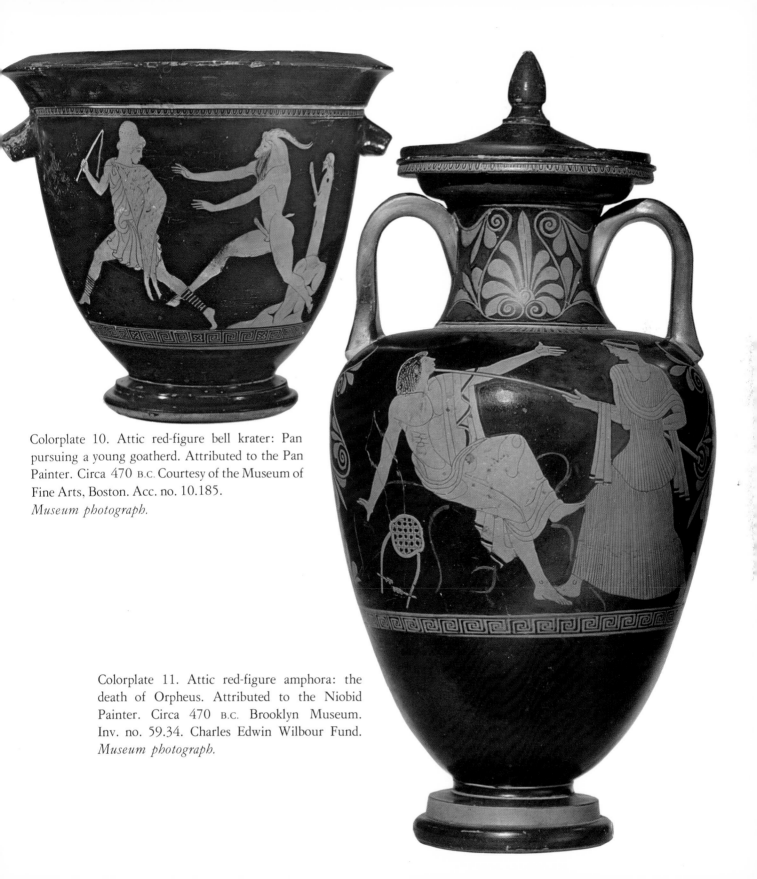

Colorplate 10. Attic red-figure bell krater: Pan pursuing a young goatherd. Attributed to the Pan Painter. Circa 470 B.C. Courtesy of the Museum of Fine Arts, Boston. Acc. no. 10.185. *Museum photograph.*

Colorplate 11. Attic red-figure amphora: the death of Orpheus. Attributed to the Niobid Painter. Circa 470 B.C. Brooklyn Museum. Inv. no. 59.34. Charles Edwin Wilbour Fund. *Museum photograph.*

Colorplate 12. Attic white-ground lekythos: woman at tomb. Attributed to the
Reed Painter. Late 5th century B.C. Leon
Pomerance Collection, New York. *Photograph: courtesy of the owner.*

Colorplate 13. Attic red-figure stand figuring two sphinxes with raised wings, their heads modeled in relief. The companion piece is in the Metropolitan Museum of Art, New York. Circa 490 B.C. Norbert Schimmel Collection, New York. *Photograph: courtesy of the owner.*

Colorplate 14. Interior of Munich's black-figure cup by the painter Exekias, showing Dionysos sailing across the "wine-red" sea; dolphins leap merrily out of the water around the slender trireme, and a grapevine in full fruit entwines the mast. The leaping dolphins may refer to an episode in the so-called "Homeric" hymn to Dionysos, which describes the god's capture by Cretan pirates. Antikensammlungen, Munich.
Photograph: Max Seidel, Mitterwald.

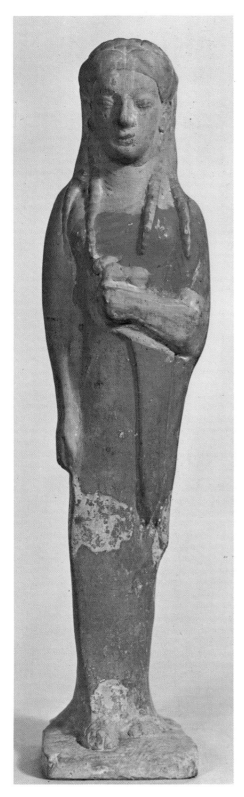

Colorplate 15. Girl holding a hare. Eastern Greek, probably Rhodian. Late 6th century B.C. Courtesy of the Trustees, British Museum, London. *Museum photograph.*

Colorplate 16. Female head, three-quarter life size. Fragmentary pinax, or votive bust. Eastern Greek, said to have been found near Knidos. Circa 500 B.C. Norbert Schimmel Collection, New York. *Photograph: courtesy of the owner.*

Colorplate 17. Pinax, or votive bust: youth (Dionysos?) holding an egg and a game-cock. From Tanagra. Boeotian. Early fourth century B.C. Courtesy of the Trustees, British Museum, London. *Museum photograph.*

Colorplate 18. Three satyr statuettes. Said to have been
found in Megara, Boeotia. Early 5th century B.C. Norbert
Schimmel Collection, New York. *Photograph: courtesy
of the owner.*

Colorplate 19. (Frontispiece) Votive ears of wheat. This unusual object was found around 1900 in a tomb near Syracuse, Sicily. Fourth to 3rd centuries B.C. Formerly in the collection of James Loeb. Norbert Schimmel Collection, New York. *Photograph: courtesy of the author.*

Colorplate 20. Snake armlet set with a central garnet in a "knot of Herakles." Said to have been found in Eretria. Formerly in the collection of Dr. Jacob Hirsch, New York. Courtesy of the Schmuckmuseum, Pforzheim. Inv. no. 1957.12. *Photograph: Gerd Wipfler.*

Colorplate 21. Dove pin. Gold, carnelian, and glass. The eyes are droplets of red glass that are not contained in settings but simply fused to the gold background. Northern Greek. Second half, 3rd century B.C. German private collection. *Photograph: courtesy of the owner.*

3

Vases

WHY COLLECT GREEK VASES?

In the early nineteenth century, to collect art meant first and foremost to assemble a cabinet of "Graecian" vases. These were installed in the library of every household that laid claim to taste and refinement, and formed the status symbol, as it were, of bourgeois cultivation. The early nineteenth-century interest in Greek vases was a literary and romantic one, based largely on association rather than on aesthetic merit. The mysterious sepulchers of Etruria, which were then just beginning to be opened and which yielded vast quantities of Greek vases, appealed strongly to an age that delighted in the morbid, and the high antiquity of the vases themselves confirmed literary notions of past perfection forever lost—in short, of the very sentiment immortalized in Keats' famous "Ode on a Grecian Urn."

The pictures on Greek vases were familiar to a generation steeped in Pindar, Ovid, and Racine. Here were the very gods and goddesses, nymphs and satyrs, that disported themselves on one's own stuccoed ceilings, that supported one's sauceboats and graced one's tureens.

With the advent of the Industrial Revolution, cabinets of Greek vases grew rarer. In a period nearly as crammed with astounding technical achievements as our Space Age, the past naturally lost some of its fascination, and antiquarian interest waned. Keats' precept ceased to be taken seriously as a means of improving the human condition. During the late nineteenth and early twentieth centuries, the Art Nouveau movement urged a break with ancient Greece and a return to nature. This trend was continued by the cult of Primitive Art that followed in the wake of World War II.

At the time of this writing, a reverse trend is clearly discernible. Greek vases are once more in demand. Their prices have doubled and tripled within the last ten years, and continue to rise. The success of Op art and Pop art are part of the same phenomenon—a reaction to the abstract and nonrepresentational—that has made the Greek vase once more a treasured and even fashionable possession.

Clearly the time would appear to be at hand to consider Greek vases afresh and to examine their present-day appeal.

First their form. The Greek potter achieved a perfection of shape, best described as "dynamic symmetry," that has never been equaled. A taste responsive to disciplined beauty (as contrasted to natural or primitive beauty) cannot but appreciate the perfect symmetry of the Greek vase.

The number of shapes are few (compared to Chinese and Japanese pottery), and each is consummately adapted to its function. There are the *amphora,* or two-handled wine and oil jar (*see* Chart "Principal Shapes of Greek Vases"), and the *krater,* in which wine and water were mixed. The *hydria* is for water, as the name implies: the horizontal handles are for lifting and setting down, the vertical central handle for pouring (and steadying when carried on the head). Among the smaller vases, the *kantharos, kylix,* and *skyphos* are various forms of drinking cups, whereas the *lekythos* was used for oil (the special mouth facilitated shaking out, rather than pouring the liquid). The *psykter* is the Greek answer to refrigeration: its graceful shape, with a low center of gravity, is so constructed that it will bob upright when filled with wine and floated (for maximum surface area in cooling) in a *krater* of ice water even when the wine, which was removed with a dipper, has been emptied. The *pyxis* was a toilet box for jewel-

Principal Shapes of Greek Vases, after G. M. A. Richter, *Handbook of Greek Art* (Phaidon Press, 1959)

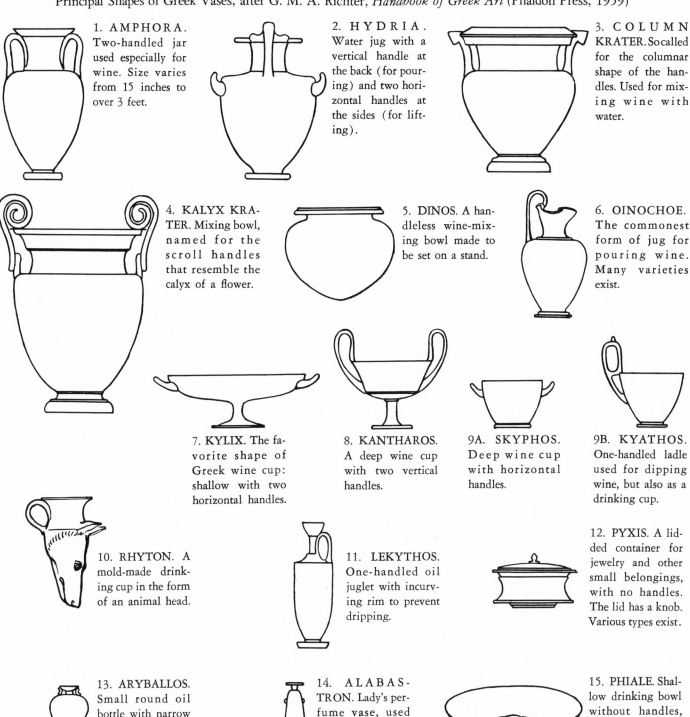

1. AMPHORA. Two-handled jar used especially for wine. Size varies from 15 inches to over 3 feet.

2. HYDRIA. Water jug with a vertical handle at the back (for pouring) and two horizontal handles at the sides (for lifting).

3. COLUMN KRATER. So called for the columnar shape of the handles. Used for mixing wine with water.

4. KALYX KRATER. Mixing bowl, named for the scroll handles that resemble the calyx of a flower.

5. DINOS. A handleless wine-mixing bowl made to be set on a stand.

6. OINOCHOE. The commonest form of jug for pouring wine. Many varieties exist.

7. KYLIX. The favorite shape of Greek wine cup: shallow with two horizontal handles.

8. KANTHAROS. A deep wine cup with two vertical handles.

9A. SKYPHOS. Deep wine cup with horizontal handles.

9B. KYATHOS. One-handled ladle used for dipping wine, but also as a drinking cup.

10. RHYTON. A mold-made drinking cup in the form of an animal head.

11. LEKYTHOS. One-handled oil juglet with incurving rim to prevent dripping.

12. PYXIS. A lidded container for jewelry and other small belongings, with no handles. The lid has a knob. Various types exist.

13. ARYBALLOS. Small round oil bottle with narrow disc-shaped mouth.

14. ALABASTRON. Lady's perfume vase, used with a dipstick.

15. PHIALE. Shallow drinking bowl without handles, generally with a central boss (omphalos).

ry and other precious belongings. These shapes were varied but little throughout their development; the Greeks valued perfection of an existing type more
than change.

Some modern critics have found the very perfection of these shapes disturbing. Thus, for example, Sir Herbert Read *(The Meaning of Art)* feels that
"there is more vitality and joy in an unsophisticated peasant pot." Obviously
the same music cannot please every ear; it is true that the Greek vase does represent the other end of the ceramic spectrum from the peasant pot and that those
gratified by the one are unlikely to be satisfied with the other.

But the greater importance of the Greek vase lies not in its shape but in its
painted decoration. In the Greek vase, and in the Greek vase alone, pottery is
elevated from a craft to the rank of major art. The drawings on Greek vases
are the first master drawings in the history of Western art. Moreover, they represent a special phenomenon: drawing on a three-dimensional surface. (Picasso
revived this peculiarly Greek approach to pottery in his series of brilliant ce-
ramographic creations at Vallauris.) Shape and decoration are wedded in harmonious union; the one is created specially for the other. For that reason Greek
vase paintings must be seen and studied in the original; they lose much of their
vibrant beauty transferred to the two-dimensional surface of a photograph, not
to mention the roll-out drawings to which archaeologists were formerly addict-
ed.

Finally, the Greek vase stands alone in the history of ceramics as a vehicle for the transmission of major pictorial content. The Greeks were at once
the most sensitive and the most intellectual race the world has ever known.
Their painted pottery was an important visual expression of their national ethos,
or "Greekness." Vases to them served more than a utilitarian purpose: they
were both religious objects—"holy pictures," as it were—and decorations not
dissimilar in their function to the pictures on our walls—Madonnas, still lifes,
photographs of sport and cinematic idols.

Myth and epic, simultaneously religious and educational, were the favorite subjects, but daily life is also documented in these vase pictures in infinite-
ly varied and extraordinarily faithful detail. The "informal" pictures in particular present us with subjects of unending fascination. The Brygos Painter's
banqueter vomiting while his favorite hetaera, or female companion, holds his
head, for example, invites comparison with Dutch and Flemish "genre" paintings. Except for works by the great masters, such as Brueghel and Vermeer,
however, Lowlands art suffers by the comparison. Its "genre" scenes, amusing

at first encounter, tend to be stereotypes and of a rather heavy humor. One misses in them the Greek vase painter's delicacy and keen psychological perception. Whereas the Lowlands painter drew on stock subjects, which he repeated ad infinitum, the Greek, fascinated by the world around him, drew on nature and rarely painted the same subject twice. He sketched youths as they exercised in the palaestra and painted prostitutes at rest as only Toulouse-Lautrec has rendered them since. Fleeting moments are recorded as on the canvases of Degas: a woman leaning over a laver to rinse her hair, a boy practicing his music lesson while an admiring companion listens. The human element in such representations makes them universal and timeless, and constitutes their highest achievement.

In his endeavor to record every aspect and nuance of human occupation, the Greek vase painter seems to have been possessed by an encyclopedic urge. The artistic record of Greek life in these creations is complete. Every conceivable pose and attitude of the human body is documented, every occupation shown. Actions that even the frankest modern artist would leave unrepresented—for the simple reason that they would not be apt to inspire him—are taken up by the Greek painter and rendered with such charming candor and originality that we are forced to acknowledge their validity as a source of art. Greek art knows no obscenity; "artistic censorship," if it existed, limited itself to forbidding the representation of sacred Mysteries.

Mention must also be made of the many representations of animals on Greek vases. The vase painter was ever fascinated by animals, and observed them keenly and sympathetically. Who will deny that the rabbit on a Greek mug in the Metropolitan Museum (Fig. 73) is worthy of comparison with Dürer's treatment of the same subject, or that the Berlin Painter's lioness (Fig. 74) is one of the finest portraits of the beast before Rubens? Even an animal sketch by an anonymous minor artist can possess infinite charm (Fig. 75).

HOW TO LOOK AT GREEK VASES

The Greek vase poses some special problems of connoisseurship. To learn to interpret the pictures on Greek vases is to learn to see. For this reason, the study of Greek vase painting is perhaps the finest training in connoisseurship obtainable.

Seeing Greek vase paintings is more than an intuitive reaction to the interplay of line and form: it is an active intellectual exercise dependent on the

Fig. 73. Attic red-figure mug in the shape of a cow's hoof. Detail: rabbit between two cows. Fifth century B.C. Courtesy of the Trustees, Metropolitan Museum of Art, New York. Acc. no. 38.11.2. Fletcher Fund, 1938. *Museum photograph.*

Fig. 74. Attic red-figure pelike-amphora, decorated by the Berlin Painter. On the neck, a lioness. Circa 480 B.C. Museo di Spina, Ferrara. Inv. no. T 867. *Photograph: Hirmer, Munich.*

Fig. 75. Pair of Attic red-figure dwarf lekythoi, decorated respectively with a panther and with a startled fawn. Unattributed. Later 5th century B.C. Possession of the author.
Photograph: Evelyn Hagenbeck.

meticulous observation of detail. To interpret is to see; to see is to be able to describe. In most cases an accurate description brings with it the correct interpretation as an inevitable consequence.

Even when drawn from classical mythology, the subject matter of Greek vase painting is very likely to be familiar. Greek myth is, after all, the basic component of Western painting before the twentieth century. When, occasionally, an obscure myth is represented, we can think of it in terms of a queer miracle represented in a beautiful medieval or Renaissance painting. Lack of familiarity with the life and miracles of the obscure saint in question will surely not blunt our enjoyment and appreciation of the painting.

More often, however, the content of a Greek vase painting will be readily accessible. Thus, for example, a young hoplite bidding his parents farewell is the soldier departing for battle in any war or in any age. Scenes of women dressing, undressing, or bathing, or scenes of courtship and lovemaking (Fig. 76), so basic to Greek vase painting, can be readily equated with basic human acts or situations—and appreciated with the same direct pleasure—as can a group of bathers or a pair of lovers by Cézanne.

Interpretation

The Homeric epics provided the Greek vase painter with his most fertile source of inspiration; hence some familiarity with them is basic to any serious study of Greek painting. Reading the *Iliad* and the *Odyssey* will provide the key to

Fig. 76. Attic red-figure oinochoe attributed to the Shuvalov Painter: couple making love. Circa 430-420 B.C. Staatliche Museen, Antiken-Abteilung, Berlin (West). Inv. no. F2414.
Photograph: Jutta Tietz-Glagow.

the interpretation of many an otherwise enigmatic picture. Beyond that, a good handbook of Greek mythology, such as the classic by Rose, can be heartily recommended.

Erudition, however, is not a prerequisite to the understanding of Greek vases. The pictures themselves provide a variety of clues to help us. The basic elements of the scene represented are usually easily definable if analyzed as we would analyze the subject of any painting. Which figures are most important? Which play a minor role? What is the action in which the figures are engaged (pursuit, assault, supplication, and so on)? Next, gesture: Careful attention to gestures can play an important role in the correct interpretation of a vase painting. Whereas today we rely largely on words and facial expressions to convey meaning, the ancient Greek (like the modern Greek) made eloquent use of his hands. Gesture, in Greek art, has its own vocabulary: it is always explicit, and frequently supplies the clue to the understanding of an action.

Attributes. Greek artists left little to guesswork. The gods, goddesses, minor deities, and heroes that appear on Greek vases are very often identified by the attributes they wear or carry. They are, as it were, the signposts to guide us. Some attributes with which we are all familiar are Zeus' lightning, Hermes' winged boots, Poseidon's trident, and Artemis' bow, but there are many others (*see* chart, pp. 139-40). The understanding of action plus the correct identification of attributes are usually all that is required for a vase interpretation. Thus, for example, a bearded figure wielding a trident and pursuing a woman can only be Poseidon chasing the sea nymph Amphitrite (as our mythological handbook will inform us if we have not already guessed).

Finally, all other signposts failing, there are the name inscriptions to help us out of our quandary. The ancient vase collector seems to have been a good deal less perspicacious than his modern counterpart, for the figures on Greek vases are often provided with labels even when their attributes make it perfectly clear who they are. We append a chart of the commonest letter forms for those unfamiliar with the Greek alphabet (p. 140). Once deciphered, it is a simple matter to look up the names in a handbook of mythology.

Having arrived at an interpretation in the manner outlined above, we may check its correctness by consulting one of several illustrated vase catalogs (*see* bibliography), which may be found in the reading rooms of most large libraries and museums. The repertory of mythological subjects represented on Greek vases is limited, and the chances are good that we can find a picture similar to ours. But let us save this "easy way out" as a final check, and learn to interpret on our own. Frequent visits to a museum possessing a large and well-labeled collection are of course the best exercise in interpretation that may be had. In the United States these are Baltimore, Berkeley, Boston, Cambridge, Cleveland, New Haven, New York, Philadelphia, and Providence. Toronto, Canada, also has a fine vase collection.

Attribution

Nearly a thousand Athenian vase painters can now be identified. The sea of Corinthian pottery has likewise been charted, and great inroads have also been made during recent years in the field of South Italian vase painting.

Among the profusion of Attic painters, great personalities stand out just as clearly as in the painting of the Italian Renaissance. Exekias, the Amasis Painter; Makron, Douris, the Brygos Painter: such names correspond to the Titians, Tintorettos, Raphaels, and Correggios two millennia later.

With few exceptions, the great Athenian potter and painter personalities flourished between 570 and 440 B.C.—the golden age of vase painting. Some signed their works (Exekias, Phintias); the great majority, however, remain anonymous, and for these an ingenious system of naming has been devised. Some have been baptized for the city or town in which their best-known work is kept, such as the Berlin Painter; others are known by recurrent or characteristic representations or idiosyncrasies of style, such as the Elbows Out Painter. Yet others are known for the place where one of their works was found, such as the Altamura Painter, and even for distinguished collectors, such as the Tyszkiewicz and Sabouroff Painters.

The scholarly classification of Athenian vase painting is largely the achievement of a British scholar, Sir John Beazley. Beazley, who has devoted a lifetime to the subject, placed the painters and potters of nearly all important Attic vases on the map of art history in two monumental works, *Attic Black-Figure Vase Painters* (1956) and *Attic Red-Figure Vase Painters* (1947; enlarged and revised edition, 1963). These serve as the twin cornerstones for the attribution of Attic vases to their potters and painters; in fact, attribution is impossible without them. Both works are a miracle of organization, and they can be profitably consulted by the novice.

It has been the author's experience, however, that collectors generally prefer to leave attribution to the specialist. Moreover, vases have generally already been attributed by the time they reach the collector (for a vase offered with a painter's name naturally fetches a higher price than an anonymous work). For this reason, we shall not go into the technique of attribution here, but refer the interested reader to the bibliography.

HISTORICAL SURVEY

Mycenaean Pottery (circa 1600 - 1100 B.C.)

The earliest vases that can be called Greek are those of the Mycenaean period. Homer's heroes were Mycenaean Greeks. These Mycenaeans, who dominated Greece from their citadels on the rich Argive plain during the latter half of the second millennium, overran Crete in about the year 1500 B.C. They transformed the old Minoan culture that had existed on the island for centuries before their arrival, while adopting, and being themselves transformed by many elements of Minoan civilization.

In the field of pottery, many of the delicate Mycenaean shapes, with their high center of gravity and elegant ribbon handles, are indebted to Minoan tradition. The most original Mycenaean contributions in the field of pottery were in the realm of decoration: the principle of abstraction keynotes later Mycenaean art. Plants, animals, and even human figures are dismembered into their various components and reassembled as a cumulation of characteristic views. There is a remarkable kinship between the Mycenaean view of nature and Cubism's revolutionary contribution to European painting in much more recent times. A Mycenaean krater in the British Museum shows two men in a chariot: the two horses are drawn the way a Cubist would draw them, with body in profile view and two highly abstract heads positioned one above the other (Fig. 77).

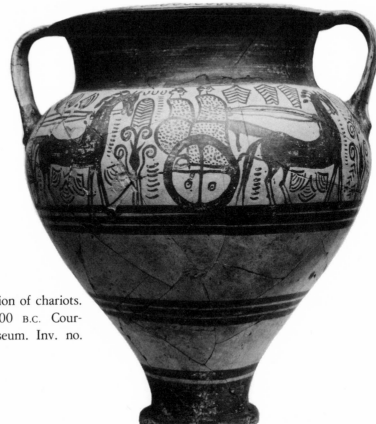

Fig. 77. Mycenaean krater: procession of chariots. From Marion, Cyprus. 1400-1300 B.C. Courtesy of the Trustees, British Museum. Inv. no. 1925.11-13.
Museum photograph.

Very characteristic shapes are the tall stemmed goblet resembling a champagne glass and the so-called "stirrup jar," a squat globular vase surmounted by twin handles and a spout for oil. A perennial favorite for the decoration of stemmed goblets was the cuttlefish with symmetrically disposed tentacles and great staring eyes (Colorplate 7). The "stirrup jars" were generally decorated more simply, with linear patterns. Other shapes of smaller vases, such as the deep bowls which Mycenaean ceramics abound in (Colorplate 8), frequently have simple animal pictures on the body. Large vessels, such as stamnoid jars and

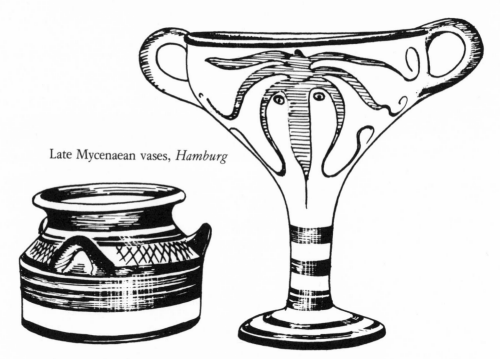

Late Mycenaean vases, *Hamburg*

kraters, often have more enterprising decorations. A Late Mycenaean krater in the Museum of Fine Arts, Boston (Fig. 78), is painted with a frieze of goats in silhouette, rendered with a whimsical slapdash that expresses the essential "goatness" of the animals to perfection. The surface of these vases is usually covered with a pale orange buff or slip, and the decoration is applied in glaze, the color of which may range from black to orange-red.

The exhibition "Early Art in Greece," held at the André Emmerich Gallery in New York (May 7 - June 11, 1965) showed a good cross-section of Mycenaean vases available at the time.

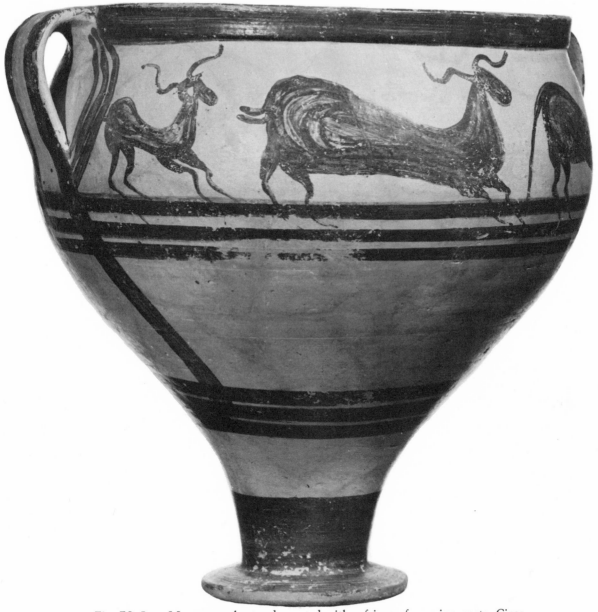

Fig. 78. Late Mycenaean krater decorated with a frieze of running goats. Circa
1250 B.C. Courtesy of the Museum of Fine Arts, Boston. Acc. no. 59.710. Otis
Norcross Fund.
Photograph: D. Widmer, Basel.

Geometric Vases (circa 1000 - 700 B.C.)

During the twelfth century B.C., northern invaders brought Mycenaean civilization to a violent end and ushered in a period of "dark ages" that lasted for
over a hundred years. Recovery was not achieved until the tenth century B.C.,
when Athens emerged as the leading center for vasemaking. During the so-
called Geometric period (circa 1000 - 700 B.C.), Greek pottery was virtually
an Athenian monopoly. Other Geometric styles, such as Cretan and Argive,
existed, to be sure, but none matched the brilliant achievement of the Attic
potters and painters.

Attic Geometric pottery represents a sharp departure from Mycenaean
ware, both in shape and in decoration. The firm and sedate forms that emerge in
this period are the ancestors of most later shapes of Greek vases—amphorae,
bowls, and pitchers—destined soon to achieve that perfection of symmetry that
is the essence of Archaic and early Classical Greek pottery.

The decoration of Geometric vases, usually fired black shading to brown,
and somewhat less lustrous than the Mycenaean, is mapped out according to
a strictly disciplined scheme. A complex system of architectural divisions—friezes, metopes, and triglyphs—embraces the vase and "interprets" its cubic form
in the manner of a geometric equation. The vessel's basic divisions are articulated by decorative zones, and these are in turn subdivided and filled with geometric ornaments, such as swastikas, meanders, lozenges, diamonds, zigzags,
and triangles. Geometric vase painting has been aptly called a "style of straight
lines and sharp corners."

Both animals and human beings are included in the Geometric scheme,
but wherever they appear they are subordinated to the geometric framework

of their setting. The favorite scenes represented concern war and funerals. On an amphora now in Karlsruhe, for example, the dead person lies in state in a panel on the vessel's neck (Fig. 79). The bier is depicted in "Cubist" fashion (as in Late Mycenaean art)—the sum total of its parts as seen from three different viewpoints. Around the deceased are assembled mourners, who make a great display of grief by raising their hands to their heads. These figures are represented the way a child would draw them, with owlish heads, triangular chests, and wasplike waists; they are shown in a juxtaposition of frontal and profile views. Below, in a frieze that embraces the waist of the vessel, passes

Fig. 79. Attic Geometric amphora decorated with a "prothesis" scene, warriors and chariots and two animal friezes. Late 8th century B.C. Badisches Landesmuseum, Karlsruhe. Inv. no. 60/12. *Museum photograph.*

Geometric pyxis

the funeral procession: chariots followed by warriors carrying shields and spears. The horses are rendered most amusingly with cylindrical bodies, dual heads, and a centipede-like array of legs.

The decoration on the oinochoes (pitchers) of the Geometric Age often focuses on horses and birds, the favorite animals of the period (Figs. 80a, 80b).

Popular forms of the smaller vases were the *kantharos* (Fig. 81) and the *pyxis*. The pyxis was a low basket-shaped container for precious belongings. Judging by the large number that have been found in tombs, these objects must have played an important role in the funeral ceremony. The most attractive type of Geometric pyxis is that in which the lid is surmounted by the statuette of a horse or sometimes by a group of horses (Fig. 82). The animals are hand-

Figs. 80a, 80b. Attic Geometric pitcher decorated with a herd of grazing mares suckling their colts, over a frieze of waterfowl, and various geometric motifs. Eighth century B.C. Museum für Kunst und Gewerbe, Hamburg. Inv. no. 1919.363.
Photograph: F. Hewicker.

modeled, and their harness is indicated in glaze. It has been suggested that the teams of horses on these pyxides have a symbolic connotation: they may represent the chariot team that drove the dead man to the grave. Some Geometric pyxides have lids surmounted by various types of intricately formed and patterned knobs including profiled disks, cones, and combinations of disks and cones. No two are alike. The attraction of these compact shapes with their beautifully articulated decoration is apparent; hence their great popularity with collectors.

Fig. 81. Attic Geometric kantharos. Middle of the 8th century B.C. Museum Antikensammlungen, Munich. Inv. no. 8501.
Museum photograph.

Fig. 82. Attic Geometric pyxis. The lid is surmounted by three horses. 8th century B.C. Museum of Fine Arts, Houston.
Museum photograph.

Orientalizing Vases (circa 720 B.C. - circa 550 B.C.)

A revolution took place in Greek vase painting at about the end of the eighth century B.C. The "straight lines and sharp corners" of the Geometric style gave way to a style of sinuous curves: angular geometric ornament disappears and exotic floral forms are substituted. This new style was ushered in as the result of contact with a foreign people. Assyrian, Hittite, Phoenician and even Urartian objects in bronze and ivory, as well as Oriental textiles, were finding their way to Greece. Greek artists, impressed by the exotic splendor of such objects, copied their ornament assiduously (hence the name "Orientalizing").

Greek vases now literally teem with animals. Ferocious beasts—lions and panthers—appear everywhere. Mythological monsters abound: sphinxes, griffins, sirens, dragons. Such creatures had long been part of the artistic repertory of the ancient Near East, but the Greeks of the seventh century must have viewed them in amazement. On an Orientalizing *olpe,* or pitcher, in the British Museum (Fig. 83) two roaring lions threaten a serpent; a fantastic double-bodied animal with a panther head, wings, and a lion's forelegs is represented in the lower register.

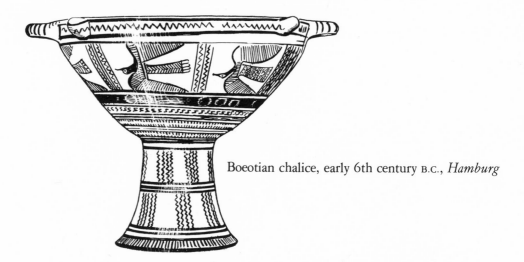

Boeotian chalice, early 6th century B.C., *Hamburg*

Fig. 83. Orientalizing olpe: snake flanked by lions, and double-bodied panther-bird. Corinthian. Circa 625-600 B.C. Courtesy of the Trustees, British Museum. Inv. no. 60 2-1 18.
Museum photograph.

Corinthian and Eastern Greek Pottery

Corinth eclipsed Athens as a pottery producer in the seventh century. Her colorful, if mass-produced, products found ready markets in the rapidly expanding Greek colonies overseas—in southern Italy and Sicily, Spain, France, Cyprus, and, in the sixth century, even on the northern shores of the Black Sea. Corinthian vases, moreover, were much admired by the Etruscans, who imported great numbers.

The development of Corinthian pottery has five main phases: Proto-Corinthian, Transitional, Early, Middle, and Late. In Proto-Corinthian (circa 725 - 640 B.C.), Transitional (circa 640 - 625 B.C.), and Early Corinthian (circa 625 - 600 B.C.) Geometric order still prevails. The figures are well spaced and are often drawn with extreme delicacy. A good example of the Transitional phase is the fine olpe in Hamburg with its registers of stately sphinxes, sirens, bulls, panthers, and stags. The filling ornaments are not incised.

In Middle Corinthian, at the beginning of the sixth century, the compositions, especially on the smaller vases, tend to get increasingly crowded, and the figures are often lost in the explosion of subsidiary ornament—mostly blobs and rosettes—with which every inch of available space of these vases is covered. The rosettes are in fact often nothing more than large blobs in which a cross or few lines have been scratched to indicate the petals, and these ornaments sometimes fill the air around the figures like shellbursts. The Dodwell Painter's oinochoe in Hamburg is a case in point.

The mechanical quality of Middle Corinthian continues in Late Corinthian (circa 575 - 525 B.C.), with the difference that the designs are now painted on an artificially prepared red background, rather than directly on the whitish surface of the clay. Small vases are most common, and they are decorated with a limited range of subjects, usually single animals. To this period belong vast numbers of *aryballoi,* small spherical containers probably exported more for their contents—unguents and scented lotions—than for their decoration. Such minor works can be found in most antiquities collections. An attractive group are the "warrior aryballoi," decorated with a row of marching soldiers, consisting of a compass-drawn shield, a head above, and two legs below.

Proto-Corinthian aryballos, *Hamburg*

Early Corinthian (Transitional) olpe, *Hamburg*

Middle Corinthian oinochoe by Dodwell Painter, *Hamburg*

Late Corinthian aryballos, *Hamburg*

Rhodian oinochoe, *Hamburg*

The islands of Rhodes, Samos, and Chios, as well as the flourishing trade emporiums along the eastern Mediterranean coast, competed with Corinth for the rich overseas market in pottery wares. Rhodian pottery is perhaps the most attractive. While the drawing is sometimes sketchy, it is always lively. Running deer and wild goats, disposed as on an Oriental textile, are the chief elements of Rhodian decoration (wild-goat style, circa 650-580 B.C.). These animals are drawn in a combination of silhouette and crisp outline style; no use is made of incision until circa 600 B.C.; the filling ornaments are thinner than in Corinthian. A certain type of squat high-necked pitcher with cloverleaf mouth and figuring a frieze of wild goats was especially popular in Rhodes during the seventh century (Fig. 84).

Corinthian and Eastern Greek plastic vases are among the most charming ceramic creations of the Orientalizing period. These small mold-made containers in the form of animals, inanimate objects, and even human beings are found in great numbers throughout the Mediterranean.

The originality of these small ceramic sculptures is often amazing. A squatting man in the Metropolitan Museum is tattooed with hedgehogs and foxes on his arms and legs. There are holes in his hands and hair for suspension (for these perfume containers were generally worn from the wrist); when a cord is drawn through the holes it becomes plain that the fellow is hogtied. Dead hares are shown as if suspended by their front paws, heads hanging back, waiting to be skinned, and deer have detachable heads that serve as stoppers. In addition there are hedgehogs, rams, toylike lions (Fig. 85), owls (Fig. 86), and panthers. They can be easily identified as Corinthian by the characteristic cream-colored clay of which they are formed.

Corinthian plastic deer and ram , *Hamburg*

Fig. 84. Orientalizing oinochoe with trefoil mouth and tripartite handle: lion and fallow deer, and wild goats. Rhodian. Middle Vlastos style, circa 635-615 B.C. Museum für Kunst und Gewerbe, Hamburg. Inv. no. 1917,988.
Museum photograph.

Fig. 85. Corinthian plastic vase in the shape of a couchant lion. Second half, 7th century B.C. National Archaeological Museum, Syracuse.
Museum photograph.

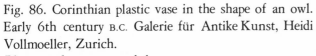

Fig. 86. Corinthian plastic vase in the shape of an owl. Early 6th century B.C. Galerie für Antike Kunst, Heidi Vollmoeller, Zurich.
Photograph: courtesy of the owner.

Eastern Greek specialties in the field of plastic vases include the helmeted head of a warrior and the bust of a demure young lady with almond eyes and a mischievous smile. Sandaled feet, entire legs, genitals, and figures of draped females also occur (Figs. 87a, 87b). The clay is generally reddish and speckled with mica.

Plastic vases in faïence were also produced in Eastern Greece (hedgehogs, grotesque heads), apparently in competition with similar Egyptian products.

Eastern Greek plastic aryballos, *Metropolitan Museum of Art, New York*

Eastern Greek faïence hedgehog, *Hamburg*

Figs. 87a, 87b. Perfume vase in the shape of a woman holding a dove. Eastern Greek or possibly Sicilian. Circa 540 B.C. Joseph Veach Noble Collection, New York.

Photograph: courtesy of the owner.

Early Attic black-figure juglet, *Hamburg*

Attic Black-Figure Vases (sixth century B.C.)

Attic black-figure vase painting is a technique of silhouette and incision. The figures were painted in black silhouette directly onto the red clay of the pot; touches of white and purple were added, and the details incised with a pointed tool before the firing.

A highly formal technique and style, Attic black-figure is apt to discourage the uninitiated by its austerity. This very quality, however, accounts for its strength, and we must try to adjust ourselves to it: black-figure is an acquired taste, like chamber music.

The very nature of the black-figure technique dictated that all figures and all actions must be reduced to clearly readable silhouettes (Fig. 88). For this reason running figures in black-figure are represented with knees and elbows bent to convey the notion of speed. Warriors advance with their right foot forward, and in a duel the victor always approaches from the right. There is little anatomy: in order to distinguish men from women the skin of the latter is painted

Early Attic black-figure kylix, *Hamburg*

Attic black-figure vases, *Hamburg*

The Technique of Attic Black-Glaze

The chemistry of Attic black-glaze, the extraordinary medium that enabled Athenian painters to lay the foundations of Western drawing 2,500 years ago, is marvelously simple. The brilliant metallic Attic "glaze" is actually not a glaze at all. It consists of nothing more than the earth of which the pot itself is made. The secret of the formula, long a mystery but now well understood (thanks largely to the research of the German ceramist Theodor Schumann), is that one and the same substance, when applied in a thin solution to the surface of a vase, can be fired both red and black: red in a well-ventilated kiln, black under reducing conditions. Red and black, moreover, can be produced on one and the same pot with but a single firing.

In chemical terms, if the amount of oxygen in the kiln is "reduced" by sealing off the supply of air at a certain point in the firing process, carbon monoxide (CO) is produced. This carbon monoxide is an unstable compound and seeks to acquire an extra molecule of oxygen wherever it can in order to form stable carbon dioxide (CO_2). In the potter's kiln, carbon monoxide will "steal" the molecule of oxygen it requires for its chemical stability from the clay surface of the pottery being fired; that is to say, the ferric oxide of the clay (Fe_2O_3 is converted into black ferrous oxide ($2FeO$)—or, expressed in a formula: $CO + Fe_2O_3 = 2FeO$. The Greek ceramist obtained both red and black on one and the same pot by employing glazes of differing concentration. One, the thinner, was low in ferric oxide, and fired ("reoxidized") red; the other, thicker, glaze failed to reoxidize in firing, and remained black.

white. These are standard conventions with which the painter overcame the limitations of his medium. Keen psychological observations are nevertheless possible in black-figure painting through the sensitive use of engraved line. Indeed, the most dramatic compositions are possible in a silhouette style (witness Picasso's "Tauromachy").

Black-figure is also unsurpassed as a medium for the rendering of metic-

Fig. 88. Attic black-figure panel amphora: Dionysos and satyrs. Third quarter, 6th century B.C. Cleveland Museum of Art. Acc. no. 27.433. A. W. Ellenberger, Sr., Endowment Fund.

ulous ornamental detail. Achilles' armor on a Boston amphora by the Amasis Painter is represented with loving precision, almost as in copper engraving. In fact, black-figure is at its best where heraldry is involved. The rampant rams on another of the Amasis Painter's amphorae in Boston are among the finest shield devices in Greek art (Fig. 89).

Severe limitations notwithstanding, Attic black-figure produced a number of notable painters. The best of these were active in the years 560 to 530 B.C., when the development of black-figure was already drawing to a close. Exekias and the Amasis Painter have long been regarded as the undisputed masters of the technique. The former achieved incredible delicacy in the handling of engraved line ("a blend of austerity and charm" [Beazley]). His best known work is undoubtedly the Dionysos cup in the Munich Antikensammlungen (Colorplate 14).

The Amasis Painter decorated both small vases and pots, but he is at his best in the former. An oinochoe by his hand in the Metropolitan Museum of Art shows two newlyweds in a donkey cart. It is in out-of-the-ordinary subjects

Fig. 89. Attic black-figure amphora signed by the potter Amasis and decorated by the Amasis Painter: warriors setting out. Middle of the 6th century B.C. Courtesy of the Museum of Fine Arts, Boston. Acc. no. 01.8026. Pierce Fund.
Museum photograph.

such as this that he reveals himself as an innovator. His most unusual work is the cup in the Schimmel Collection illustrating two scenes from the *Iliad* (Figs. 90a, 90b, 90c).

Among the most pleasing of Attic black-figure vases are the so-called "Little Master" cups, a special variety of delicate drinking bowl set on a slender stem. The lightweight fabric of which they are made often resembles bone china and rings like a glass when tapped. Most "Little Master" cups are decorated by specialized miniaturists (hence the name). Short inscriptions in the handle zone—part and parcel of the decorative scheme—often give us the artist's name ("so and so made me"). Tleson, the son of Nearchos, one of the finest potters of "Little Master" cups, signed over sixty. A Tleson fragment in Hamburg (Fig. 91) represents a grazing deer over an inscription exhorting to "Hail and drink!" The beautiful Little Master cup signed by Tleson in the Boston Museum has a splendid five-point stag, mortally wounded by a hunter's spear, in its roundel (Fig. 92). Another charming Little Master was recently acquired by the Richmond, Virginia, Museum (Fig. 93).

We cannot abandon the subject of Attic black-figure without at least a brief mention of Nikosthenes, the potter who put his signature to most of the many vases of "Nikosthenic" shape to have survived. Nikosthenes, in addition to having an obvious passion for signing his name, was also one of the most prolific and original potters of the later sixth century. Characteristic "Nikosthenic" shapes include neck amphorae of a special variety (with flaring rims developing into wide ribbon handles—a deliberate copy of an Etruscan shape, for the

Figs. 90a, 90b, 90c. Attic black-figure cup (kylix) by the Amasis Painter. On one side (90b), Poseidon's stable is represented. The façade is decorated with a series of metopes representing various animals—lions, monkeys, and partridges—in meticulous miniature. Below, two grooms attend Poseidon's horses, nervous, aristocratic animals, while the god's golden imps disport themselves on the animals' backs. On the other side of the cup (90c) Poseidon himself sees the two Ajaxes (*Iliad* 13, 39ff.) off to the Trojan wars. We may admire the beautiful shield emblems—a ram and the protome of a lion—for these are the Amasis Painter's specialty in which he obviously took great delight. Circa 540 B.C. Norbert Schimmel Collection, New York.

Fig. 90a

Photograph: courtesy of the owner.

Fig. 90b

Fig. 90c

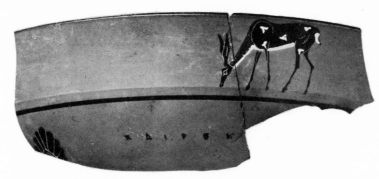

Fig. 91. Rim fragment of a black-figure lip cup by the Tleson Painter: grazing deer. Inscribed CHAIRE KAI P[IEIN]— "Hail and drink!" Middle of the 6th century B.C. Museum für Kunst und Gewerbe, Hamburg. Inv. no. 1967. 34. *Museum photograph.*

Fig. 92. Black-figure lip cup signed by the potter Tleson and decorated by the Tleson Painter: wounded stag. Middle of the 6th century B.C. Courtesy, Museum of Fine Arts, Boston. Acc. no. 98.920. Pierce Fund. *Museum photograph.*

Fig. 93. Black-figure lip cup: on both sides, a solitary panther turns his head to face the beholder and raises his paw. Below, "nonsense inscriptions," a jumble of Greek letters that make no sense at all. Middle of the 6th century B.C. Virginia Museum of Fine Arts, Richmond. Acc. no. 62-1-14.

Etruscan market), cups, skyphoi, and pyxides. Although generally carelessly decorated, the shapes of these vases are engaging and their pictures often entertaining, as, for example, the cup signed "Nikosthenes epoiesen" ("Nikosthenes made it") in the Berlin Museum (Fig. 94). The potter Nikosthenes employed a number of painters in his workshop, of whom the most talented is known as the "BMN Painter" (for "British Museum Nikosthenes").

With such works, the black-figure style is pushed almost beyond its limits. The curtain is about to rise on a new development: Attic red figure.

Fig. 94. Attic black-figure cup signed by the potter Nikosthenes. Interior teems with figures: the conventional roundel contains a seated sphinx; around her are grouped pairs of fighting cocks interspaced by hens, a frieze of training athletes (wrestlers, boxers, footracers, javelin thrower, discus thrower), and an outer frieze of goats, panthers, deer, and two spread-winged sphinxes. Third quarter, 6th century B.C. Staatliche Museen, Antikenabteilung, Berlin (West). Inv. no. F1805.
Photograph: Jutta Tietz-Glagow.

Attic Red-Figure Vases (fifth century B.C.)

A revolutionary discovery, around the year 530 B.C., transformed the history of ceramic art, and produced the finest paintings on clay the world has ever known. The idea was simple enough: a reversal of the black-figure (that is, black-on-red) color scheme. Instead of painting the figures black, it was now the background that was blackened. The figures were "reserved," or left in the natural color of the clay, thereby opening the way for line drawing with a brush.

The Technique of Attic Red-Figure

1. Red ocher is rubbed into the unfired surface to be painted, which is then polished.

2. A preliminary sketch is made, using a pointed instrument.

3. The figures are laid on in heavy glaze outline (the so-called glaze "contour lines" that are clearly visible in a raking light).

4. The background is filled in.

5. Details are drawn within this red-on-black negative silhouette employing a special glaze of high viscosity. The lines, known as "relief lines," stand off from the clay background; one can feel their relief with one's fingers.

6. Fine details, stippling, and the like, are added in diluted glaze. Some use—much more sparing than in black figure—is also made of red and white accessory color.

7. The vase is fired (see p. 109).

Whereas black-figure was described as a style of silhouette and incision—basically an engraver's technique—red-figure is truly a technique of drawing. The emancipation of line that the invention of red-figure permitted marks no less paramount a development in the history of art than the discovery of true linear perspective two thousand years later. Able at last to vary the thickness of his line and to produce an effect of shading, the painter was now encouraged to abandon age-old conventions and to strike out in new directions. Athenian vase paintings from the end of the sixth century B.C. and the beginning of the fifth

abound in experimentation. One painter places a figure with one leg in profile and the other frontal, in an effort to suggest the third dimension; another
shows a naked figure from behind. Painters vie with one another in producing
ever more daring anatomical renderings, such as the naturalistically depicted
profile eye or the human back in foreshortened view.

Athenian vase painters of the fifth century must have been continuously swapping ideas, for the over-all picture that is presented by the development
of Attic red-figure is one of smooth, uninterrupted progress and shared achievement. During the earlier black-figure period, Greek vase painting had fallen
behind the other arts, notably sculpture, as a medium for the expression of revolutionary artistic ideas. Now it is once more in the avant-garde. It is intriguing
to observe the gradual but inexorable liberation of the drawn line that takes
place during the fifth century, to watch the problems of form and space being
neatly solved. So rapid is the progress toward naturalism and total freedom of
line that it can be calibrated virtually decade by decade.

It is easy, with a bit of practice, to scan the development of Attic red-figure
in the mind's eye and to date these vases accurately. Look at the heads of the
figures; the drawing of the eyes is particularly revealing. The almond-shaped
frontal eye of Attic black-figure gradually becomes asymmetrical, with the inner
and outer corners differentiated. After about 500 B.C. the pupil begins to move
toward the inner corner, and toward 475 B.C. the inner corner opens to suggest
a profile view. The true profile eye is achieved in the second quarter of the century; and with this development the way for the recording of the human emo-
tions through facial expressions lies open (in black-figure, emotion could be
suggested only by pose and gesture). Hair is another good index to the date of
a red-figure painting. At the beginning—from circa 530 to 500 B.C.—it is rendered according to the simple black-figure scheme: a black mass set off from
the black background by an incised line. After circa 500 B.C. it is set off by a
"reserved" red line with a fringe of curls along the edge. Gradually however,
the locks of the fringe lengthen and begin to follow the contour of the skull.
Finally, toward the middle of the fifth century, the "black mass" scheme is abandoned altogether, and the hair is rendered in separate strands drawn with dilute
glaze.

Other chronological indications to watch are the development of musculature and drapery, both of which follow their own evolution from black-figure
convention to truly "free" and naturalistic forms.

Great strides forward are also made during this age in the combination of figures into groups and in their naturalistic spatial interrelations (Colorplate 13). Figures in action had always interested the Greek painter. With the new tools at his disposal, he is now able to produce complicated action studies such as were previously impossible. A case in point is the Berlin cup attributed to Douris (Fig. 95), on each side of which a group of six merrymakers is represented. Through subtle grouping, an atmosphere of festive animation is achieved. The naked bodies of the high-stepping and pirouetting dancers set off against

Fig. 95. Attic red-figure drinking cup (kylix) attributed to Douris: revelers. Circa 490-480 B.C. Staatliche Museen, Antikenabteilung, Berlin (West). Inv. no. F2289.
Photograph: Jutta Tietz-Glagow.

their opened cloaks are an absorbing study in point and counterpoint motion. One senses the rhythm of the music.

Attic red-figure can be conveniently divided into three phases: Late Archaic (circa 530-480 B.C.), Severe Style (circa 480-450 B.C.) and Free Style (second half of the fifth century B.C.). The styles of most of the more than five hundred red-figure vase painters that have been charted are so individual that it has been possible to reconstruct workshops and to trace master-pupil relationships. Great painters inevitably have their epigones. While it is hardly possible to give even a thumbnail sketch of the most outstanding painter-personalities in these pages (for a fuller discussion, see the bibliography at the end of this chapter), I should nevertheless like to acquaint the reader with a few names.

The Late Archaic period is, as we have said, an experimental phase, and the paintings of this period possess the naïveté and wide-eyed enthusiasm of pioneer art. Among the finest painters devoting themselves to the decoration of drinking cups and small vessels in this period (others specialize in the decoration of pots) are **Onesimos** and **Epiktetos,** of whom Beazley has written "You cannot draw better; you can only draw differently." Both excelled in inventing novel motifs to fill the roundel of a kylix. The kneeling satyr holding a drinking horn, in the Boston Museum (Fig. 96), is a fragmentary masterpiece that admirably characterizes the experimental spirit of the age. The artist was concerned first and foremost with the challenge imposed by a circular composition, second with recording the muscular transitions of a body seen in contrapostal view. Even though the representation of the foreshortened leg is not wholly successful, we cannot but admire the daring and originality of the conception.

Fig. 96. Central roundel from an Attic red-figure drinking cup (kylix) attributed to Epiktetos: satyr holding a drinking horn. Circa 500 B.C. Courtesy of the Museum of Fine Arts, Boston. Acc. no. 10.212. James Fund and Special Contribution.
Museum photograph.

Oltos, another painter of cups and small vases, is easily recognizable by his jagged masculine style. Among his finest works are two psykters, or wine coolers, in the Metropolitan Museum and in a New York private collection (Colorplate 9). The Metropolitan vessel is decorated with a group of young athletes exercising in the presence of their trainers. No two athletes are seen in the same position, and the figures have something of the self-conscious air of an anatomy demonstration by Vasarius. The unique artistry of the second psykter lies in the inventive novelty of the conception. Six armed hoplites carrying spears and beautifully emblazoned shields ride around the midriff of the vase on dolphins. When the vessel was filled with wine and floated in a krater full of ice water, the dolphins swam on the surface—that is to say, they would appear to leap from the depths and submerge again as the psykter bobbed in the cooling liquid. Note the red inscription EPIDELPHINOS ("dolphin rider") beside each figure.

The **Brygos Painter** is the supreme master of frenzied movement. His favorite subjects are the revel—human revel as well as the orgies of satyrs and maenads—and the pursuit. The Boston kantharos showing Zeus pursuing Ganymede (Fig. 97) is typical for his animated style. Healthy boys with strong chins engaged in sport (Figs. 98a, 98b) are a perennial favorite.

Attic red-figure juglet, *Hamburg*

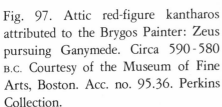

Fig. 97. Attic red-figure kantharos attributed to the Brygos Painter: Zeus pursuing Ganymede. Circa 590-580 B.C. Courtesy of the Museum of Fine Arts, Boston. Acc. no. 95.36. Perkins Collection.
Museum photograph.

Figs. 98a, 98b. Attic red-figure skyphos attributed to the Brygos Painter: athletes. Courtesy of the Museum of Fine Arts, Boston. Acc. no. 10.176. Perkins Collection.
Museum photograph.

Compared with the Brygos Painter, **Douris** might be considered somewhat of an academician were it not for the great originality with which his calm and slow-moving figures are conceived. Although he seems to have been active over nearly half a century (over two hundred vases are attributed to him), the majority of his paintings, including his best works, seem to fall in the decade 490-480 B.C. Two women folding and putting away their clothes, on the interior of a cup in the Metropolitan Museum (Fig. 99), show the artist as a keen observer of life and as an accomplished anatomist (one of the women is seen in a difficult contrapostal view). There is little trace of archaism in the quiet classicism of this carefully balanced composition. With Douris, Attic red-figure has fully matured.

The other great master of the early fifth century is the **Berlin Painter.** Like Douris, he bridges two generations and two styles. His early works stand squarely in the Archaic tradition; his late phase foreshadows the classicism of the Periclean age. Like a number of his contemporaries, the Berlin Painter decorated both large and small vases. His most celebrated pots include his namepiece in Berlin and a monumental amphora (height 26½ inches) acquired a few years ago by C.I.B.A. (Basel), a Swiss drug-manufacturing concern. The latter can probably lay claim to being the most dearly purchased Greek vase in existence. The Berlin amphora figures Apollo and his fawn accompanied by Hermes; on the Basel amphora, Athena and Herakles are shown. A characteristic small work by the Berlin Painter was recently acquired by the Berlin Museum (Figs. 100a, 100b): an oinochoe showing Nike crowning an athlete. Both the large amphorae and the small oinochoe adequately illustrate the master's unmistakable stylistic hallmarks: monumental figures splendidly isolated against their black surroundings; long, eloquent glaze lines combined with almost miniaturist attention to detail.

Among the mannerists active in this period, painters who consciously retain the quaintness and grace of the Archaic style, the **Pan Painter** is justly the best known. He is named after a bell krater in Boston on which the ithyphallic goat-man Pan pursues a young shepherd, who glances back in a mixture of fear and fascination (Colorplate 10). "The forms are old but the spirit is new and highly individual" (Miss Richter).

The most noteworthy masters of the Severe Style are the **Sotades Painter** and the **Penthesilea Painter.** The former, one of the most prolific talents of his age, decorated unusual shapes, such as lathe-fluted bowls, cups with wishbone handles, and head vases, often with small, graceful figures flying along at great speed (Fig. 101). His inimitable satyrs can never be mistaken for the work of another painter—unless it be one of his own pupils.

Fig. 99. Attic red-figure drinking cup (kylix) attributed to Douris: two naked women putting down their clothes. Circa 470 - 460 B.C. Courtesy of the Trustees, Metropolitan Museum of Art, New York. Acc. no. 23.160.54. Rogers Fund, 1923.
Museum photograph.

Figs. 100a, 100b. Attic red-figure oinochoe attributed to the Berlin Painter: Nike offering an athlete a crown. Circa 480 B.C. Staatliche Museen, Antikenab-teilung, Berlin (West). Inv. no. 1965.5
Photograph: Susanne Mauss.

The Penthesilea Painter is a spontaneous and sensitive draftsman. His finest works are decorated in polychrome colors on a white ground, such as the double-faced disk in the Metropolitan Museum (a toy?) decorated with Zephyr and Hyacinth on the one side and Victory crowning an athlete on the other. A cup in Hamburg is characteristic of his average, less imposing production: youths with their horses are represented on the exterior and a boy reciting his music lesson to a friend on the interior (Figs. 102a, 102b, 102c). The dignified serenity of these paintings is typical for the Penthesilea Painter, whose style can easily be recognized by a number of characteristic physiognomic details, especially the delicate pointed noses, the pouting lips, and the wavy hair.

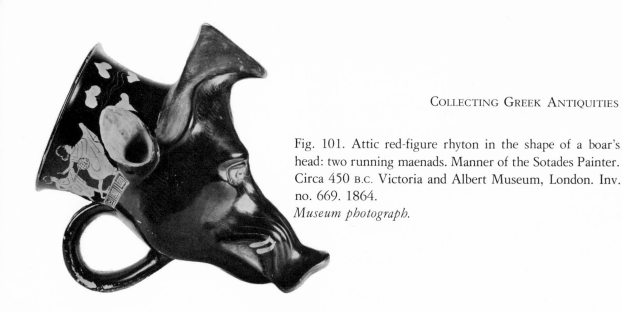

Fig. 101. Attic red-figure rhyton in the shape of a boar's head: two running maenads. Manner of the Sotades Painter. Circa 450 B.C. Victoria and Albert Museum, London. Inv. no. 669. 1864.
Museum photograph.

Figs. 102a, 102b, 102c. Attic red-figure drinking cup (kylix) attributed to the Penthesilea Painter. Exterior (102a, 102b): ephebes with their horses. Interior (102c): two boys, one seated holding a lyre. Museum für Kunst und Gewerbe, Hamburg. Inv. no. 1900.164.
Photograph: F. Hewicker.

Fig. 102a

Fig. 102b

Fig. 102c

Attic white-ground lekythos, *Hamburg*

Mention might also be made of the **Niobid Painter,** for an excellent work of his has recently entered the Brooklyn Museum. The subject of Brooklyn's new amphora (Colorplate 11) is the death of the rhapsode Orpheus, who according to tradition was torn to pieces by the angered Thracian women, whose husbands had been seduced by his music. In this majestic work, Orpheus has sunk to the ground; although he feebly tries to defend himself against the onrushing woman brandishing a spit for roasting meat, his end is obviously at hand. Works such as this reflect some of the grandeur of contemporary easel and fresco paintings, known to us mainly from descriptions by classical authors.

The last phase of Attic red-figure vase painting, known as Free Style, presents little that is new. Sotades seems to have had a profound influence. His stylistic tradition is carried on by a number of talented minor artists such as the **Eretria Painter,** whose pictures have some of the fleeting quality of Zen.

There is also much careless work in the second half of the fifth century. The pupils and followers of the Penthesilea Painter in particular can be indicted for what amounts to mass production. The decline of red-figure is briefly arrested toward the end of the century by the appearance of the **Meidias Painter,** whose virtuoso style was continued into the early fourth century by a series of hacks, the "sub-Meidians" (Fig. 103). The chief interest of these vases lies in their representation of myth. At the same time a number of painters (**Jena Painter, Q Painter),** notorious for their wretched drawing, appear on the scene. With them, Attic red-figure has run its course.

One special development of Greek vase paintings remains to be considered: the *white-ground lekythos.* These slender oil vessels did not serve any practical purpose and therefore did not need to be durable. Sometimes they were placed in the tomb beside the body; sometimes they were brought to the tomb as offerings by the family of the dead. The perishable white-ground technique, by which matte colors—blue, red, yellow, and green—were applied to a chalky ground, was apparently considered most appropriate for funerary dedications. The subjects of white-ground lekythoi are also inevitably sepulchral: a tomb being dec-

Fig. 103. Attic red-figure acorn lekythos: seated woman holding a phiale; facing her is a standing man holding a mirror. "Sub-Meidian." Fourth century B.C. Landesmuseum für Kunst und Kulturgeschichte, Oldenburg. Inv. no. 6775. *Museum photograph.*

orated for the festival of the dead (Colorplate 12), the boatman Charon fetching a passenger for the voyage across the river Styx, and so on. The noble and restrained style of these vases is superbly evocative of resignation and silent grief—Greek sorrow as it is expressed also by the marble stelae (see p. 11). Regrettably, the beautiful polychromy has often disappeared, leaving in many instances only the glaze outlines of the figures.

Other shapes of Greek vases were decorated in the white-ground technique, but they are rarely encountered (Fig. 104).

The number of preserved Attic black- and red-figured vases is tremendous: more than 25,000 have been registered to date, and the actual number of existing specimens must constitute a substantially larger figure. With hundreds of Greek vases being unearthed each year, this obviously is one of the richest and most rewarding areas still open to today's collector.

Hellenistic Pottery

The quality of Greek painted pottery declined rapidly after 400 B.C.; consequently, fourth-century Attic is apt to disappoint the collector whose perceptions have been nurtured on the high standards set by Greek potters and painters during the preceding two centuries. The dying out of Athenian painted pottery does not, however, mean the end of Greek ceramics.

The Hellenistic period (circa 300 - 100 B.C.) is the age of relief pottery. Relief wares—either entirely mold-made or with a molded relief applied to a wheel-made body—take over where painted pottery leaves off. These products generally imitate vessels of precious metal such as were very popular throughout the Greek world in the Age of Alexander, and not infrequently they were actually manufactured with the aid of molds taken from metal originals. After the death of Alexander in 323 B.C., the process of artistic decentralization initiated during his lifetime was accelerated. The Greek world separated, and a

Fig. 104. Attic white-ground alabastrum (perfume vase): on one side, Nike holding a bird and a scepter; on the other, a victorious athlete. Circa 480 B.C. Staatliche Museen, Antikenabteilung, Berlin (West). Inv. no. F2258.
Photograph: Jutta Tietz-Glagow.

number of mutually exclusive kingdoms were established. Each royal residence naturally attracted artists to it, and several "schools" soon flourished. The most important of these were Alexandria in Egypt, Antioch in Syria, Pergamon in Asia Minor, and the Island of Rhodes. Each of these centers, in addition to several others, produced pottery of a special variety.

Alexandrian faïence, decorated with beautiful impressed designs of Oriental character, is highly prized by collectors. Intact specimens are quite rare owing to the fragile nature of the material, but even good fragments can be collector's items. Characteristic shapes are hemispherical bowls (Figs. 105a, 105b), pitchers, and drinking horns. The attractive brownish *Megarian bowls* (Fig. 106) are fairly common on the other hand. Their metallic-looking molded decorations consist, as a rule, of acanthus leaves and floral scrolls developing from a central rosette at the bottom of the bowl. Well fired and of tough clay, these vessels have not infrequently survived intact.

Pergamene Relief Ware, made of a reddish clay and found throughout western Asia Minor, is similar to the "Megarian" but of somewhat coarser quality. Large plates and bowls with stamped decorations are characteristic. Because of the low quality of the average specimen, this ware is not apt to attract the

Figs. 105a, 105b. Faïence bowl. Alexandrian. E. Kofler-Truniger Collection, Lucerne.
Photograph: courtesy of the owner.

advanced collector. Quite different however, is the case of so-called *Calenian Ware,* made, as we now know, not in Cales (Campania, South Italy) but in Tarentum, the "Athens of Magna Graecia" on Italy's heel. Calenian bowls, plates, askoi, and gutti (a very characteristic shape resembling a Roman lamp but with a long spout on the shoulder [Fig. 107]) are readily identifiable by the fine metallic sheen of their black glaze and by the high quality of their relief decorations—again, frequently taken from metal originals (in some cases from coins already a century old). Important examples of Calenian relief pottery, such as the

Fig. 106. Krateriskos and hemispherical bowl. Megarian. Third to 2nd centuries B.C. Museum für Kunst und Gewerbe, Hamburg. Inv. no. 1917,990, 1917.176.
Photograph: Evelyn Hagenbeck.

Fig. 107. A so-called guttus: two seated nymphs holding musical instruments. "Calenian" ware. Tarentine. Early 3rd century B.C. Jatta collection, Ruvo di Puglia. Inv. no. J880.
Photograph: courtesy of the German Archaeological Institute, Rome.

relatively rare drinking cups decorated in the middle with the cast of a Syracusan decadrachm coin representing the head of the nymph Arethusa surrounded by dolphins, are prized even by the most discerning of collectors.

South Italian Pottery

To return once again to painted pottery, we now arrive at the last flowering of the art. Attic vase painting had already entered the slump preceding its final eclipse when this craft was in the process of being developed in the Greek colonies of South Italy. South Italian vase painting is almost entirely red-figure, and most of it dates from the second half of the fourth century B.C. The earlier examples, of about 380-350 B.C., are still dominated by Attic conventions and traditions. Gradually, however, the local potters and painters of South Italy achieved independence. Several regional styles can be distinguished, notably those of Lucania, Campania, Paestum, Apulia, and Sicily. For the purpose of this brief collector's survey we shall confine our remarks to Apulian—at once the most pleasing and the most plentiful of the Italiote potteries. First, the shapes: whereas the pottery shapes of other South Italian centers are apt to be monotonously repetitive, the ceramic workshops of Tarentum in Apulia were busily experimenting and turning out a great variety of original and attractive shapes. Two of the most characteristic shapes found in Tarentine pottery and hardly elsewhere are the *epichysis* and the *rhyton.* The former is a squat beaked jug (Fig. 108) that seems to have been most popular, the latter a molded beaker in the form of an animal head (Fig. 109). Other shapes, such as the *situla* (a ritual bucket), imitate metal prototypes, and sometimes their handle attachments are decorated with reliefs cast or copied from metal originals. Fish plates and platters were another local specialty, although these are found in Campanian ware as well. Several complete services—a large deep platter with vertical handles and a set of matching smaller plates with a central cavity (for olive oil?)— have been sold in the last few years, all apparently from fresh excavations. These fish dishes are decorated on the inside with a most fascinating variety of creatures of the deep: perch, flounders, squid, mollusks, tunnyfish, devilfish, dolphins—an entire menu of gourmet delights from fourth-century Magna Graecia (Figs. 110a, 110b).

One suspects that most of these Apulian painted vases (contrary to the very common unpainted "household wares") were never used by the living and that their purpose was exclusively sepulchral. The reason for this assumption is that

Fig. 108. Epichysis. Tarentine. Third quarter of the 4th century B.C. Museum für Kunst und Gewerbe, Hamburg. Inv. no. 1875.66.
Museum photograph.

Fig. 109. Rhyton in the shape of a griffin head. From Ruvo. Tarentine. Third quarter of the 4th century B.C. Courtesy of the Trustees, British Museum. Inv. no. WT 317.
Museum photograph.

Figs. 110a, 110b. Fish platter. Tarentine. Middle of the 4th century B.C. Norbert Schimmel Collection, New York.

Photograph: courtesy of the owner.

the pictures on Apulian—indeed on all South Italian vases—refer to death and the afterlife in nearly every instance. Fourth-century South Italy was a spawning place for mystery cults promising a life in the hereafter. Dionysiac Orphism was but one of several religions that promised its adherents everlasting bliss in the company of the satyrs and nymphs. This typically Hellenistic preoccupation with death is reflected in the thematic repertory of South Italian vases. The smaller vessels—kantharoi, oinochoi, rhyta, and the like—will very often represent a single male or female figure, probably a generalized representation of the dead person, seated on a rock, standing, or striding along carrying various types of cult paraphernalia—libation vessels (sometimes stacked three or four, one on top of the other), thyrsoi (the mystic emblem of Dionysos), musical instruments, fans, grapes, wreaths, and so on. Sometimes a rather effeminate-looking Eros is shown flying along carrying one or more of these implements; sometimes he stands and hands them to the departed (Fig. 111). Typical for this form of representation is the scene figured on an oinochoe recently on the Swiss art market on which the "blessed departed" attend the wine-god Dionysos and mingle with satyrs in a light-footed dance (Figs. 112a, 112b, 112c).

Mention must be made of the literally thousands of Apulian vases of every conceivable shape that figure simply a female head in profile, sometimes flanked by wings, at other times emerging from a leafy calyx (Fig. 113). Obviously a goddess of the underworld is represented, but her exact identity remains unknown.

Fig. 111. Two skyphoi: Eros and woman. Tarentine. Third quarter, 4th century B.C. ("Ornate Style"). Jatta Collection, Ruvo di Puglia.
Photograph: courtesy of the German Archaeological Institute, Rome.

Figs. 112a, 112b, 112c. Oinochoe (Shape 3: chous). Dionysiac scene: Dionysos, women, and satyr. A dwarf stands to the left. Tarentine. Middle of the 4th century B.C. By the Felton Painter. Formerly Basel market (Münzen & Medaillen A.G.).
Photograph: Dietrich Widmer.

Fig. 113. Footed alabastrum: Satyr head emerging from a leafy calyx. "Gnathia" ware. Tarentine. Middle of the 4th century B.C. Jatta Collection, Ruvo di Puglia. Inv. no. J1235.
Photograph: courtesy of the German Archaeological Institute, Rome.

No discussion, however brief, of South Italian pottery can conclude without a mention of *"Gnathian" vases,* named after the Apulian town of Egnazia, where large numbers were found in the last century and where it was formerly thought that they were produced (they are, in fact, all Tarentine). "Gnathia," probably the output of one or two specialized Tarentine ateliers, is a polychrome technique as well as a style. White, yellow, and purple on a background of black glaze are its colors. Grapes and grape leaves, as well as scrolls, necklaces, and ribbons, are favorite ornamental devices. The figure decoration of "Gnathian" vases, often exquisite, employs advanced tricks of shading, using dilute glaze over a white (on black) ground. Female heads, birds, musical instruments, and Erotes are commonly depicted; on the better "Gnathian" vases these subjects are rendered with the precision of miniature painting.

Finally, a concluding word in praise of South Italian (especially Apulian and Campanian), *black-glaze pottery,* vases whose glory consists entirely in elegance of shape accentuated by the sheer luxury of lustrous glaze (although

their surface is often ribbed or fluted to give the impression of metal) (Figs. 114, 115). At their best these works are apt to be veritable tours-de-force of the potter's craft, and worthy of comparison with the best of Attic black-glaze pottery produced a century earlier. At a time when the cult of glaze is making such inroads among contemporary potters, it is surprising that Italiote black-glaze ceramics have not yet really been "discovered" by collectors. This brings us back to collectors and collecting, and to some practical considerations. As the cemeteries of Central Italy, so rich in Attic vases, are gradually being exhausted after two hundred years of incessant exploitation, attention (read "clandestine excavation") is once more shifting to South Italy. South Italian Greek vases, though popular with nineteenth-century collectors, are, with the possible exception of plastic vases, currently still neglected. I know of no private collector specializing in the South Italian field at the time of writing, although the prices are still relatively low, and the material is both rewarding and available.

Fig. 114. Kantharos. Campanian black-glaze. Fourth to 3rd centuries B.C. Museum für Kunst und Gewerbe, Hamburg. Inv. no. 1897,220. *Museum photograph.*

Fig. 115. Oinochoe (Shape 3: chous). Tarentine black-glaze. Fourth to 3rd centuries B.C. The handle terminates at the top in a ram's head; the head of Medusa is figured in relief at the lower attachment. Formerly Basel market (Münzen & Medaillen A.G.). *Photograph: Dietrich Widmer.*

SOME ATTRIBUTES OF MYTHOLOGICAL FIGURES FREQUENTLY REPRESENTED ON GREEK VASES

Gods and Goddesses

Aphrodite	Draped or naked; generally accompanied by one or more Erotes
Apollo	Frequently holds lyre, or bow and arrows; bearded in black figure—later beardless
Artemis	Huntress: bow and arrows; dog
Athena	Owl; snake; most frequently armed with lance and shield
Dionysos	Grapes, wine cup or drinking horn; frequently accompanied by satyrs and maenads
Eros	Youthful god, naked and winged
Helios	Haloed charioteer
Hephaistos	Hammer, short chiton, sometimes a blacksmith's cap
Hera	Draped goddess, generally with crown and scepter
Hermes	*Petasos* (traveling hat), winged boots, caduceus (snake scepter)
Nike	Winged goddess, often carries a libation bowl, a pitcher, or a victor's wreath
Poseidon	Trident, dolphin, more rarely tunnyfish
Zeus	Lightning, scepter; always bearded

Heroes

Achilles	Shown as a hoplite; common in black-figure
Dioskouroi	(Castor and Pollux) Conical hats *(pilos);* generally shown with their horses
Herakles	Lionskin, club, bow and arrows; represented engaged in labors, resting, holding the apples of the Hesperides. The most popular hero represented on Greek vases
Odysseus	Usually wears a conical hat *(pilos)*
Paris	Wears pointed Phrygian cap and, frequently, long-sleeved Phrygian garments
Perseus	Cap of darkness, winged boots; frequently carries a sickle-shaped pruning knife and sometimes the head of the Medusa (in a sack)
Theseus	Hunter with short cloak and two spears; frequently represented engaged in labors (compare Herakles), most frequently slaying the Minotaur

Others

Amazons   Armed females, often mounted. They wear short skirts or long-
            sleeved Phrygian garments, and generally do battle with bows
            and arrows or hatchets

Maenads   Female attendants of Dionysos; often represented carrying the
            attributes of the god, in the company of satyrs.

Scythians   Northern barbarians, generally represented as archers, often with
            horses, wearing tight-fitting trousers and "Scythian" caps.

THE GREEK ALPHABET

Alpha	A	α
Beta	B	β
Gamma	Γ	γ
Delta	Δ	δ
Epsilon	E	ϵ
Zeta	Z	ζ
Eta	H	η
Theta	Θ	θ
Iota	I	ι
Kappa	K	κ
Lambda	Λ	λ
Mu	M	μ
Nu	N	ν
Xi	Ξ	ξ
Omicron	O	o
Pi	Π	π
Rho	P	ρ
Sigma	Σ	σ
Tau	T	τ
Upsilon	Υ	υ
Phi	Φ	ϕ
Chi	X	χ
Psi	Ψ	ψ
Omega	Ω	ω

SELECT BIBLIOGRAPHY

GENERAL

Arias, Shefton, Hirmer, *History of Greek Vase-Painting* (Munich: Hirmerverlag, 1965). Good text; excellent illustrations, many in color; useful especially for Attic.

R. M. Cook, *Greek Painted Pottery* (London: Methuen, 2nd ed., 1966). A good general account with ample bibliography.

Corpus Vasorum Antiquorum (CVA). An international catalog series embracing most of the major collections and many of the minor. The British and recent German fascicules are best. Useful for locating comparative material.

E. Pfuhl (transl. by J. D. Beazley), *Masterpieces of Greek Drawing and Painting* (New York: Macmillan, 2nd ed., 1955). A reliable account with good illustrations.

MYCENAEAN

A. Furumark, *Mycenaean Pottery: Analysis and Classification* (Stockholm, 1941). Fundamental study, indispensable to the specialist but otherwise rather dry reading.

CORINTHIAN

D. A. Amyx, *Corinthian Vases* (Berkeley: University of California Press, 1943).

A. D. Lacy, *Greek Pottery in the Bronze Age* (London: Methuen, 1967).

H. G. Payne, *Necrocorinthia* (New York and London: Oxford, 1931). Still the fundamental study of the subject. Out of print.

ATTIC

J. D. Beazley, *Attic Black-Figure Vase Painters* (New York and London: Oxford, 1956). The monumental catalog, with 10,000 entries, subject, and museum indexes forms the point of departure for any investigation of black-figure.

———, *Attic Red-Figure Vase Painters* (New York and London: Oxford, 2nd ed., 1963). The complete catalog of red-figure, with 21,000 entries.

———, *Attic Red-Figured Vases in American Museums* (Cambridge, Mass., 1918). Excellent reading. Useful especially for visits to the Boston and New York collections. Out of print.

———, *The Development of Attic Black-Figure* (Berkeley: University of California Press, 1951). A concise, lucid, and most readable account. Out of print.

J. V. Noble, *The Techniques of Painted Attic Pottery* (New York: Watson-Guptill, 1965). The most complete and up-to-date technical discussion.

G. M. A. Richter, *Attic Red-Figured Vases, a Survey* (New York and London: Oxford, rev. ed., 1958). An extremely useful sketch of the development.

G. M. A. Richter and D. F. Hall, *Red-Figured Athenian Vases in the Metropolitan Museum of Art* (New Haven, 1936). The fundamental catalog of a comprehensive collection. Good discussion of the major red-figure painters. The foldout drawings are indispensable for stylistic analyses of related works.

G. M. A. Richter and M. Milne, *Shapes and Names of Athenian Vases* (New York, 1935). Although long out of print, still the fundamental work on the subject. The illustrations of various shapes are drawn largely from the Metropolitan Museum collection.

MYTHOLOGY

R. Graves, *The Greek Myths* (Pelican Books A509, 1955).

H. J. Rose, *Handbook of Greek Mythology* (3rd ed., London, 1945). Still unsurpassed for clarity and reliability.

4

Terra-Cottas

Terra-cotta sculptures afford the collector a unique opportunity to acquire Greek originals at prices well below those of classical sculptures in other media. Indeed, a Greek terra-cotta can sometimes be purchased at less than the price of a modern imitation!

TECHNIQUE

To help the collector understand the artistic possibilities of molded terra-cotta sculptures, we shall briefly outline the steps involved in their creation. First, the coroplast, or modeler, had to make a patrix, or positive prototype. This was modeled and carved like any clay sculpture, using the fingers and simple wooden tools. Projections and deep undercutting had to be avoided in order to ensure that the figurine would separate cleanly from the mold. Projecting parts were added freehand to the finished product. Next, one or more molds were taken from the patrix. For a flat idol (Fig. 116) or a relief, a single mold sufficed. For a simple figure in the round, a front mold and a back mold were required. For a complicated "Tanagra" (Figs. 117a, 117b, 117c, 117d) several piece molds

Fig. 116. Boeotian female idol. First half 6th century B.C. Staatliche Antikensammlungen, Munich. Inv. no SL 74.
Museum photograph.

Figs. 117a, 117b, 117c, 117d. Tanagra figurines. First half 4th century B.C. Museum für Kunst und Gewerbe, Hamburg. Inv. no. 1896.461.
Photograph: Ralph Kleinhempel

145

for each projecting part had to be employed. Often, impressions from several molds—heads, arms, legs, and so on—were interchanged, permitting almost infinite variety without extra expenditure of time or effort.

When the mold had been fired and was ready for use, a slab of soft clay was spread from the center to the edges, left to dry, and then removed. Assembly of the various parts of a figure was achieved by scoring the surfaces to be joined with a sharp tool, brushing them with diluted clay (known as "slip"), and gently squeezing them together. The figurine constructed in this fashion was then ready to be fired. It will be noted that the larger Greek terra-cotta figures, including the famous Tanagras, generally have a square or oval "window" cut into the back: this is to permit the escape of air during the firing process, and thus prevent bursting.

Nearly all Greek terra-cottas were originally painted. Purple, red, blue, yellow, and green, as well as black and white, were the standard colors. Since they were generally not fired but applied as a wash to the finished product, they have in most instances disappeared. With rare exceptions only those terra-cottas fortunate enough to have survived the centuries in a dry climate such as that of Egypt or South Russia have kept much of their original color. We must therefore be wary of terra-cottas that have a well-preserved painted surface. The color is quite apt to be modern—as, often, is the terra-cotta itself. (See Chapter 8.)

ARCHITECTONIC TERRA-COTTAS

Greek terra-cottas fall into two main categories by their function: architectonic terra-cottas, comprising the clay revetments and other decorations of buildings, and figurative terra-cottas, comprising statuettes and other small portable objects. Architectonic terra-cottas are most commonly found in regions where marble is scarce, such as South Italy and Sicily, but beautiful examples are also known from the Greek mainland, especially Corinth. Under the broad rubric "architectonic" are included decorative elements as diverse as acroteria, beam ends, rainspouts, metopes, friezes, and even pedimental sculptures. The best-preserved examples come from the seismic zones of southern Italy and Sicily (Fig. 118), where a sudden earthquake might cause an entire temple to be shaken to the ground; however, a number of fine early specimens that have entered public and private collections in recent years are known to have been found

Fragmentary archaic temple revetment,
Private Collection

Fig. 118. Female head (of a sphinx?). Fragment of an architectural decoration. From Metapontum, South Italy. Circa 520 B.C. Musée du Louvre, Paris. Inv. no. CA 1793. Another fragment from the same temple decoration is in the Metropolitan Museum of Art, New York.
Museum photograph.

in western Anatolia (Turkey). Buried in debris, the terra-cotta decorations remained protected from the elements until unearthed by a clandestine digger or by an archaeologist.

Lion-head waterspouts form a most attractive type of architectonic terracotta of the Archaic and Classical periods, the finest examples coming from Sicily, and dating from the last decades of the sixth century B.C. The lion's mouth is generally wide open in a snarl with the tongue extended. These temple decorations were all once brightly painted, and the preservation of their color is of course an important consideration in establishing their value. Although quite fragmentary, an Archaic Gorgo antefix (Fig. 119) recently fetched a high price in a Lucerne auction sale on account of the unbroken freshness of its painting. The monster's curly hair, eyes, and brows are black, the lips and cheeks a brownish red. The Gorgo being of female sex, her flesh is painted white according to the Archaic convention (cf. pp. 108-109).

Fig. 119. Gorgoneion. Fragment of an architectural antefix. From South Italy or Sicily. Later 6th century B.C. Formerly on the art market, Lucerne.
Photograph: courtesy Ars Antiqua A.G., Lucerne.

FIGURATIVE TERRA-COTTAS: HISTORICAL SURVEY

Most Greek figurative terra-cottas are domestic or decorative objects that were also dedicated in temples and shrines and placed in tombs. Some were made specifically as votive dedications.

Mycenaean Period

The earliest Greek terra-cottas to have survived in quantity date from the Mycenaean Age (fourteenth to twelfth century B.C.) and are among the most charming and desirable of minor objects that can still be collected. Small figures of human beings and animals are the most common, but there are also sculptured representations of furnishings, such as tables and chairs. The human figures, nearly always female, comprise two main types: those with spherical midsections and those with upraised arms (Fig. 120). Both generally have small disk-shaped breasts and are decorated with wavy stripes in black, brown, or or-

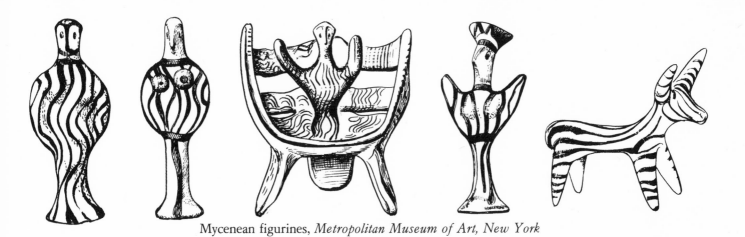

Mycenean figurines, *Metropolitan Museum of Art, New York*

Fig. 120. Two late Mycenean idols. Circa 1400-1200
B.C. Museum für Kunst und Gewerbe, Hamburg. Inv.
no. 1928,206a,b.
Museum photograph.

ange glaze. Less common are the female figures installed on a throne, probably the Mycenaean mother goddess, as well as the chariot terra-cottas, such as the fine example in the British Museum (Fig. 121).

Mycenaean animal terra-cottas include bulls, goats, dogs, and stiff-legged deer. Their vivacious spontaneity endear these works particularly to the collector attuned to the aesthetics of modern sculpture.

Archaic Boeotian Terra-Cottas

Easily confused with these Mycenaean figurines are the more plentiful (and therefore somewhat less valuable) creations produced more than half a millennium later in Boeotia. Like their Mycenaean counterparts, the Boeotian terra-cottas also consist of abstract idols and of animals. Among the former, Boeotian "board-shaped" idols are most readily identified. They have a flattened body, stumplike arms, a large protruding nose, a tall cylindrical headdress, and generally a large scroll or curl over the forehead. The body flares at the bottom to provide a base. In Greece, these figures are known as *pappades,* or "priests," for the resemblance of their cylindrical hats to those still worn by the orthodox priesthood. Seated idols are also common (Fig. 122). Both the standing and the seated

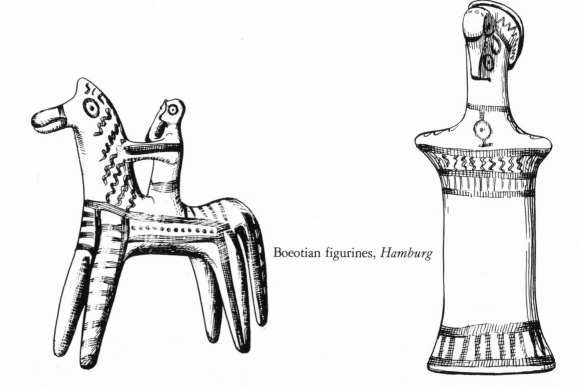

Boeotian figurines, *Hamburg*

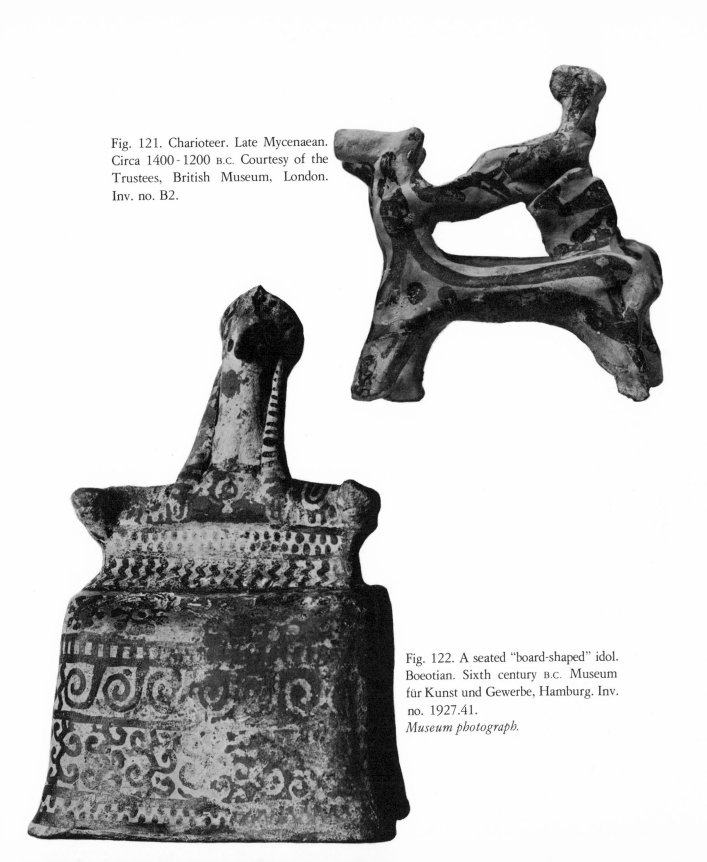

Fig. 121. Charioteer. Late Mycenaean. Circa 1400-1200 B.C. Courtesy of the Trustees, British Museum, London. Inv. no. B2.

Fig. 122. A seated "board-shaped" idol. Boeotian. Sixth century B.C. Museum für Kunst und Gewerbe, Hamburg. Inv. no. 1927.41.
Museum photograph.

are generally painted with simple designs in black and red (crisscross pattern, lozenges, scrolls, and so on). Occasionally these idols can be quite elaborate, such as the example in Boston with added details in clay and complicated painted design (Fig. 123).

Rider figurines, hand-formed in one piece with their mounts, are another attractive Boeotian type (Fig. 124). Some of these spirited little equestrians apparently held wooden spears, for their raised fists are pierced for the insertion of a slender object. Excavations in the Archaic necropolis of Rhitsona in Boeotia have established that male burials generally contain a rider figurine, whereas the grave of a woman is apt to contain one or more board-shaped female idols.

Boeotian animal sculptures include the entire range of the Greek barnyard: bulls, horses, pigs, roosters, dogs. A mother dove or waterfowl nursing her brood, in the Boston Museum (Fig. 125), is a charming variation.

Whereas Boeotian terra-cottas are by far the most plentiful for the Archaic and Classical periods, other regions of Greece also possessed terra-cotta industries.

Fig. 123. Standing Goddess. Boeotian. Sixth to early 5th centuries B.C. Courtesy of the Museum of Fine Arts, Boston. Acc. no. 01.7763. Purchased by contribution.

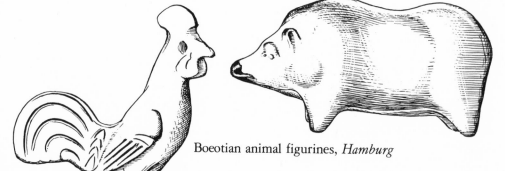

Boeotian animal figurines, *Hamburg*

Fig. 124. Statuette of a rider. Boeotian. Later 6th century B.C. Norbert Schimmel Collection, New York.
Photograph: courtesy of the owner.

Fig. 125. Dove or waterfowl with brood. Boeotian. Fifth century B.C. Courtesy of the Museum of Fine Arts, Boston. Acc. no. 35.59. Gift of Mrs. Charles Gaston Smith's Group.
Museum photograph.

Archaic Attic Terra-Cottas

Noted for their superb proportions and dignified simplicity (inviting comparison with monumental marble sculptures), the quality of Attic terra-cottas is generally high. A favorite type shows a goddess seated on a stately throne (Fig. 126). Her diadem merges in an unbroken curve with her veil, which flows gracefully over her shoulders, hands, and knees, smoothing and blending the transitions. Others show a goddess or a female worshiper standing. The serene lady in the Hamburg Museum (Fig. 127) is marked by the same tectonic balance that characterizes her seated counterparts.

Archaic Cretan Terra-Cottas

These date mostly from the second half of the seventh century B.C., the so-called "Dedalic" period. The favorite type is the votive *pinax* (Greek for "picture"), pierced at the top and obviously made to be suspended. Cretan pinakes comprise relief figures of standing females wearing tall headdresses *(poloi)*, their arms pressed tightly to their sides (Fig. 128), naked youths, and warriors. Male busts and heads are also common (Figs. 129a, 129b). These small relief sculptures have triangular faces with prominent noses, and their hair is generally arranged in a stepped "peruke." A more elaborate Cretan terra-cotta head, in Hamburg, is modeled fully in the round and therefore probably part of a statuette (Fig. 130).

Terra-cotta *pithoi*, or giant storage vessels, are another Cretan specialty, and a considerable number decorated with reliefs have survived (Figs. 131, 132). Quantities of this interesting material, mostly in very fragmentary condition, have appeared on the antiquities market of late.

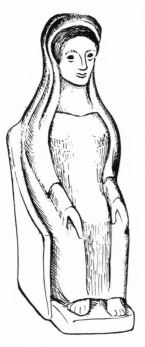

Attic votive figurine, *Hamburg*

Fig. 127. Standing goddess. Attic. Middle of the 5th century B.C. Museum für Kunst und Gewerbe, Hamburg. Inv. no. 1960.117.
Museum photograph.

Fig. 126. Seated goddess. Attic. Middle of the 5th century B.C. Museum für Kunst und Gewerbe, Hamburg. Inv. no. 1927.37.
Museum photograph.

Fig. 128. Pinax in the form of a goddess wearing a tall headdress *(polos)*. Cretan. Seventh century B.C. Museum für Kunst und Gewerbe, Hamburg. Inv. no. 1937.11.
Museum photograph.

Figs. 129a, 129b. "Dedalic" pinakes: heads of youths. Cretan. Seventh century B.C. Courtesy of the Museum of Fine Arts, Boston. Acc. nos. 26.286 and 63.465. John Wheelock Elliott Fund, 1926; gift of the author, 1963.
Museum photograph.

Fig. 130. Head of a youth. Cretan. Late 7th century B.C. Museum für Kunst and Gewerbe, Hamburg. Inv. no. 1962.16.
Museum photograph.

Fig. 131. Neck of a pithos decorated with reliefs figuring sphinxes. Cretan. Seventh century B.C. Collection of Franz Rutzen, Mainz.
Photograph: Dietrich Widmer.

Fig. 132. Fragment from a pithos: two confronting sphinxes. Cretan. Seventh century B.C. Private collection, Tokyo.
Photograph: Dietrich Widmer.

Eastern Greek votive figurines, *Hamburg*

Archaic Rhodian and Eastern Greek Terra-Cottas

Favorite types include both standing and seated goddesses, sirens (Figs. 133a, 133b), water birds, and representations of pomegranates (Fig. 134) and other fruit that were placed in the tomb as offerings, and similar objects were also fashioned to serve as plastic vases (cf. Figs. 87a, 87b). The human figures are characterized by the same plumpness that distinguishes Ionian marble sculptures. The figures tend to have Oriental physiognomies (oval faces with high cheekbones and almond eyes). Whereas the rendering of the anatomy is generally kept to a minimum, fussy attention is sometimes paid to ornamental details.

Figs. 133a, 133b. Siren. Western Greek, perhaps made with an imported Rhodian mold. Last quarter, 6th century B.C. Basel art market. *Photograph: Dietrich Widmer.*

One of the most engaging varieties represents a girl with carefully chiseled nose, almond eyes, and hair elegantly arranged in a series of long braids hanging over her shoulders (Colorplate 15). She stands barefoot and holds a hare to her breast while gracefully lifting a fold of her long garment with the other hand. Figures such as this were produced in quantity and widely exported in antiquity, and there are many examples of the type in private and public collections. Rhodian terra-cotta pinakes sometimes attain near-monumental proportions (Colorplate 16).

Rhodian and Eastern Greek terra-cottas were imitated in Sicily and South Italy. Clandestine excavations in these regions in recent years have uncovered large numbers of locally made standing and seated female figures in the Rhodian style (Fig. 135). In Gela and in Agrigento (Sicily) a standing female holding a piglet by the hind legs probably represents an earth goddess bringing a victim to the sacrifice.

Fig. 134. Votive quince or pomegranate. Probably 5th century B.C. Leon Pomerance Collection, New York.
Photograph: courtesy of the owner.

Fig. 135. Goddess or worshiper. Sicilian Greek (Gela). Middle of the 5th century B.C. Basel art market.
Photograph: Dietrich Widmer.

Fifth-Century Terra-Cotta Sculptures

These are among the most desirable collectors' items in the repertory of ancient art. The various types of seated and standing goddesses known from the
preceding Archaic period continue, but their forms now display a greater degree
of naturalism. Subjects taken from daily life become more common, and a number of novel and unorthodox representations are added to the artistic repertory.
An example of these changes is the naked hetaera, or professional entertainer,
reclining languidly on a bed or divan (Fig. 136), probably one of the first representations of the nude female in a Greek terra-cotta. The figure, an Attic work,
dates probably from the second or third quarter of the fifth century B.C.

The largest number of surviving fifth-century Greek terra-cottas again
comes from the province of Boeotia. Groups depicting daily activities such as
plowing, cooking, and breadmaking are among the earliest instances of "genre"
in Greek art. Particularly engaging examples are to be found in the Museum of
Fine Arts, Boston. These types also exist in pinax form (Colorplate 17).

Whereas such "genre" groups are archaeological rarities, other types of
fifth-century Boeotian terra-cottas are more readily available. These include the
many figures of a standing youth holding a gamecock (Fig. 137) and his female
counterpart, the elaborately coiffed girl, sometimes holding her jewel box (Fig.
138), and the god Hermes, the guardian of dead souls (Fig. 139). Such figures,
which often retain considerable traces of their ancient polychromy applied over a
white "engobe," or primer, are nearly always found in tombs (accounting for
their excellent preservation). Animal figurines, again predominantly bulls, pigs,
and roosters, were the votive dedications of Boeotian farmers.

Satyr terra-cottas seem to have been a specialty of both Corinth and Boeotia. Attic examples also exist, but they are rare. Among the finest of their type
are a group of four in a New York private collection (Colorplate 18). These
"tripodic" satyrs disport themselves in a variety of amusing poses, each supported by his tail. Similar but smaller versions are not uncommon. Related to the
satyr terra-cottas are a great variety of Boeotian and Corinthian figurines representing monkeys engaged in various human activities, such as riding, tum-
bling, and performing various antics (Fig. 140).

To the fifth century B.C. belong two important groups of small terra-cotta reliefs, apparently the inlays of wooden chests, coffins, or other tomb furniture. One (the earlier in date) comes from the Aegean island of Melos, the other
from Locri in South Italy. Owing to their high quality, both are cherished collectors' items.

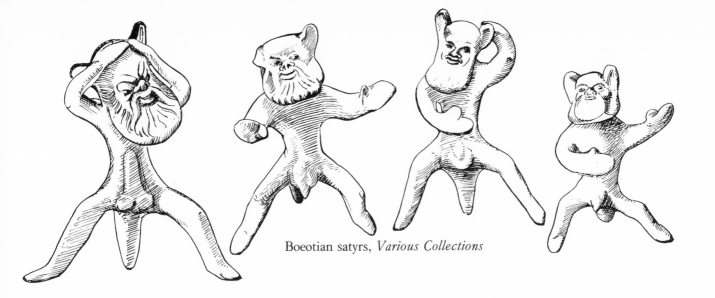

Boeotian satyrs, *Various Collections*

Fig. 136. Reclining hetaera, or courtesan. Attic. First half, 5th century B.C. Museum für Kunst und Gewerbe, Hamburg. Inv. no. 1917.399.
Museum photograph.

162

Fig. 137. Youth holding a gamecock. Boeotian. Second half, 5th century B.C. Museum für Kunst und Gewerbe, Hamburg. Inv. no. 1917.222. *Museum photograph.*

Opposite, left
Fig. 138. Standing girl with large coiffure. Boeotian. Second half, 5th century B.C. National Museum, Copenhagen. Inv. no 6346. *Photograph: Lennert Larsen.*

Opposite, right
Fig. 139. Hermes holding a ram. From Thebes. Boeotian. Second half, 5th century B.C. National Museum, Copenhagen. Inv. no. 5387. *Photograph: Lennert Larsen.*

Fig. 140. Monkey riding on a donkey. Corinthian or Boeotian. Fifth century B.C. Courtesy of the Museum of Fine Arts, Boston. Acc. no. 49.49. John M. Rodocanachi Fund.
Museum photograph.

The celebrated "Melian" reliefs, flat plaques modeled on the front only, generally figure subjects drawn from Greek mythology: Bellerophon slaying the chimera, Phryxos on the ram, the death of Actaeon, Meleager hunting the Calydonian boar (Fig. 141), and such.

Locri reliefs are more specifically votive in character. They consist largely of subjects relating to the legend of Persephone (Fig. 142), the chief South Italian deity of the underworld.

Another important source of Greek fifth-century terra-cottas is ancient Taras—modern Taranto—Sparta's flourishing colony on the heel of Italy. Tarentine reliefs continue to appear on the market in a seemingly inexhaustible supply. It would appear that their purpose, too, was exclusively funerary. The most common type represents the idealized dead person reclining on a kline,

Tarentine terra-cottas (Dionysos; heroized departed),
Hamburg

Fig. 141. "Melian relief": Meleager and the
Boar. Second half, 5th century B.C. Private
collection.
Photograph: W. Heyden, Hamburg.

Fig. 142. Relief figuring Persephone and worship-
ers. From Locri, South Italy. Fifth century B.C.
Museo Nazionale. Reggio di Calabria.
Museum photograph.

or banqueting couch (Fig. 143). He generally wears a wreath, and is draped from the waist down; occasionally he holds a rhyton or phiale, the emblem of his immortality. Representations of Dionysos, the principal divinity of the Tarentine funerary cult, also abound (Fig. 144). The soft fluid style of Tarentum can hardly be mistaken.

Mention must be made also of the Tarentine gilt terra-cotta reliefs that originally decorated Tarentine wooden tomb furnishings. Their subjects are again primarily Dionysiac and funerary. Real and imaginary animals are represented stalking one another or—in the case of griffins—attacking Arimasps (a legendary people of the Far North) (Fig. 145). These delicate and spirited works take us down to the late fourth century B.C.

Fig. 143. Head of a banqueter. Tarentine. Later 5th century B.C. Courtesy of the Museum of Fine Arts, Boston. Acc. no. 31.6 Harriet Otis Croft Fund.
Museum photograph.

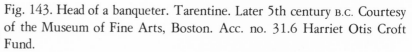

Fig. 144. Bearded bust from a reclining figure, representing the god Dionysos or a mortal banqueter. Tarentine. Later 5th century B.C. Museum für Kunst und Gewerbe, Hamburg. Inv. no. 1917.460.
Museum photograph.

Fig. 145. Gilt terra-cotta relief: Arimasp attacked by two griffins. Applique from a wooden sarcophagus. Tarentine. Third quarter, 4th century B.C. D. and J. de Ménil Collection, Houston, Texas.
Photograph: courtesy of the owners.

Tanagra Figurines

The fourth and third centuries B.C. are the era of the Tanagra figurine par excellence. These graceful, gaily colored creations were the rage of Europe when they were first illicitly unearthed nearly a century ago (near the Boeotian town after which they are named). They represent women and girls, some standing quietly in mannequin poses, displaying their elegant robes to best advantage (see Figs. 117a - 117d), others dancing (Fig. 146) or engaging in girlish games (Fig. 147). A delightful example in Hamburg shows an old Silenus carrying a young girl on his back (Fig. 148)—the Greek version of Beauty and the Beast. Another, also in the Hamburg Museum, shows a schoolgirl intently preparing her lesson (Fig. 149). Gay and cheerful as they are, such statuettes were greatly admired throughout the Greek world, and the style soon spread beyond Greece proper, to South Italy, Sicily, and beyond.

South Italian "Tanagras" are somewhat heavier and coarser than the Greek originals (Fig. 150), and their market value is accordingly lower. Before buying a Tanagra it is therefore advisable to try to establish whether it is Attic, Boeotian, or perhaps South Italian.

Tanagra figurine, *Hamburg*

Fig. 146. Dancing girl. Tanagra figurine. Fourth century B.C., or later. Museum für Kunst und Gewerbe, Hamburg. Inv. no. 1908.247.
Museum photograph.

Fig. 147. Girl playing ball. Tanagra figurine. Fourth century B.C., or later. Museum für Kunst und Gewerbe, Hamburg. Inv. no. 1896.463.
Museum photograph.

Fig. 148. Papposilenos carrying a girl on his back. Attic or Boeotian. Fourth century B.C. Museum für Kunst und Gewerbe, Hamburg. Inv. no. 1927.40. *Photograph: F. Hewicker.*

Fig. 149. Schoolgirl preparing her lesson. Tanagra figurine. Fourth century B.C., or later. Museum für Kunst und Gewerbe, Hamburg. Inv. no. 1898.53. *Museum photograph.*

170

Fig. 150. Girl seated on a rocky knoll. South Italian (Canosine?).
Late 4th or 3rd centuries B.C. Museum für Kunst und Gewerbe,
Hamburg. Inv. no. 1917.1428.
Museum photograph.

Hellenistic Terra-Cottas

The Greek East also produced terra-cotta sculpture during the Hellenistic
period, but with few exceptions it has not been possible to localize the various regional styles. Such is the case with the many small grotesques—phallic
hunchbacks (Fig. 151), burlesque actors (Fig. 152), and the like—which the
Hellenistic world delighted in. These engaging sculptures, which seem to have
been valued as *apotropaea*, or warders-off of evil, are found throughout the eastern Mediterranean. Some see in them the product of Alexandrian workshops;
others claim the Gulf of Smyrna as their home. The great quantities of terra-
cottas found in the necropolis of Balikesir near Troy (Fig. 153), that have been
finding their way onto the antiquities market in recent years, would appear to
have been locally produced.

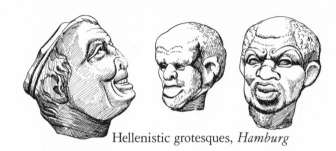

Hellenistic grotesques, *Hamburg*

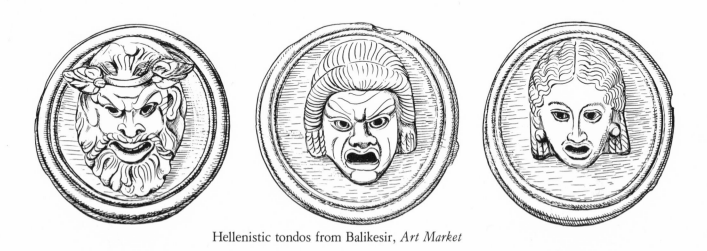

Hellenistic tondos from Balikesir, *Art Market*

Fig. 151. Hunchbacked slave. Hellenistic. Museum für Kunst
und Gewerbe, Hamburg. Inv. no. 1954.135.
Museum photograph.

172

Fig. 152. Burlesque actor. Hellenistic. Museum für Kunst und Gewerbe, Hamburg. Inv. no. 1898.52. *Photograph: F. Hewicker.*

Fig. 153. Roundel *(imago clipeata)* with the head of the god Serapis in high relief. Said to have been found at Balikesir, near Troy, together with three theater masks (see drawings on this page). When last seen by the author, the masks were on the New York art market. Late Hellenistic. Museum für Kunst und Gewerbe, Hamburg. Inv. no. 1962,125. *Museum photograph.*

PHYSICAL CHARACTERISTICS
OF GREEK TERRA-COTTAS

Attica

Orange or yellowish-brown in color. Finely textured. Difficult to distinguish from Tarentine.

Boeotia

Color usually yellow ocher, pale orange, or brownish, sometimes gray. Usually lightly fired. Fine in texture down to circa 500 B.C., thereafter coarser. Mica sometimes present in small quantities.

Corinth

Easy to recognize because of the extremely fine texture. The color, cream to pale orange.

Rhodes

Usually coarsely textured, reddish-brown in color and containing mica, which sparkles when held in a raking light.

Crete

Usually lightly fired. The clay is very fine-grained and pale orange with a cream surface; it is very often encrusted with a thin layer of chocolate-brown earth.

Tarentum

Fine in texture, similar to Attic in color but paler and containing much fine mica.

Sicily

Coarse and slightly micaceous. Color, pale orange shading to light greenish-gray.

SELECT BIBLIOGRAPHY

R. A. Higgins, *Catalogue of the Terracottas in the Department of Greek and Roman Antiquities, British Museum,* I. (London: 1954). The scholarly catalog of one of the largest and finest terra-cotta collections in existence.

————, *Greek Terracottas* (London: Methuen's Handbooks of Classical Archaeology, 1967). Distributed in the USA by Barnes & Noble, Inc. The first comprehensive handbook on Greek terra-cottas in the English language. Well illustrated, informative, and very readable. Gives a complete bibliography for the subject, including museum catalogs and excavation reports.

G. M. A. Richter, *Handbook of Greek Art* (New York: Phaidon Press, 1959). Contains a short but well-written account of terra-cottas, with bibliography.

T. B. L. Webster, *Greek Terracottas* (Harmondsworth, 1950).

F. Winter, *Die Typen der figurlichen Terrakotten* (Berlin and Stuttgart, 1903). The standard reference work for the typology of Greek terra-cotta figurines. Arranged by period, region, and subject matter, with hundreds of small drawings. Out of print, but can be consulted in the larger museum reference libraries.

The important collections of Greek terra-cottas in Boston and New York are still largely unpublished. Much information can, however, be gleaned from the handbooks of the two collections: *Greek, Etruscan and Roman Art,* The Classical Collections of the Museum of Fine Arts, Boston, 1963; G. M. A. Richter, *Handbook of the Greek Collection,* Metropolitan Museum of Art, New York, 1953.

5

Jewelry

Greek jewelry appeals to a fairly wide group of collectors. Evidence: the 1965 loan exhibition "Greek Gold," held at Boston, Brooklyn, and Richmond, which was able to draw on private collections for over half of the objects displayed (for the catalog, see bibliography at the end of this chapter).

The special appeal of Greek jewelry is easily accounted for by the extraordinarily high quality of the material. Like Greek vases, Greek jewels tend to transcend the confines of minor art: they can often be considered as miniature sculptures—much like the jewelry of the Italian Renaissance. Representations of gods and goddesses, as well as of the various sacred animals, abound; such jewels undoubtedly often had specific religious connotations.

There is a problem of display, however. Whereas some collectors feel that jewelry ought to be worn, not exhibited, and (shun it for that reason), others, fearful of theft, keep it hidden away in locked drawers or vaults. The fact is that Greek jewelry is no more or less valuable and susceptible to theft than other classes of classical antiquities. The value resides entirely in the art-content (the

175

precious-metal content being, with few exceptions, minimal). Considered from this aspect, special security precautions become meaningless: there is no reason why Greek jewelry should not be displayed in vitrines, and enjoyed exactly as other antiquities. Gold and silver mingle beautifully with works of art in other media, especially terra-cotta. The most effective jewelry displays I have seen mixed gold with terra-cotta and bronze objects in cases of fairly intimate dimensions. Neutral or pastel-colored cloth case linings are to be recommended (both silk and velvet work very well). Lucite mounts are best, for they do not distract the eye. Case lighting is essential.

I wish to discourage the wearing of original ancient jewelry, which is fast becoming fashionable. Being metallurgically very pure, Greek gold is soft and susceptible to damage. The excellent jewelry reproductions produced by the firm of Zolotas are better suited for wearing than are the precious originals.

A surprisingly large amount of jewelry has survived from antiquity, thanks to the universal ancient custom of burying some of a person's most precious possessions with him after his death. Since there were no bank accounts, gold jewelry was the ultimate tangible evidence of worldly achievement. This concept of gold is still alive today in Arab countries, where the family wealth is often worn around the woman's neck, wrists, and ankles in the form of jewelry. Beyond its obvious "investment value," however, jewelry was, and still is, coveted for its sheer luxury and beauty. In Greek mythology, Eriphyle betrayed her husband for the sake of a necklace; a finger ring set with a beautiful gemstone was the downfall of the tyrant Polykrates.

It might be well to say a few words about the materials employed by the ancient goldsmith. In addition to gold and silver, a natural alloy of these two metals resembling white gold, and known as electrum, was in use in antiquity. During the fifth and fourth centuries, gold possessed the warm "golden" color familiar to us from the jewelry of our own age. During the Hellenistic period, however, a paler, more yellowish, color prevailed. In addition to gold and silver, precious stones were also occasionally employed. For the Greeks, however, fine jewelry meant primarily high-quality workmanship. Opulent display was alien to Greek taste (this in contrast to the jewelry of the Romans, for whom gold and silver was essentially a setting for ever larger and more costly stones).

The types of jewelry worn in Greek antiquity correspond remarkably closely with those in fashion at the beginning of the last century, the period of "Classical Revival." Necklaces, earrings, and bracelets were, of course, the most common jewelry articles (the bracelets being worn both at the wrist and on the upper arm). Diadems, often with pendants, were frequently donned on festive occasions such as weddings and religious observances. Some types, of thin gold, were apparently never worn by the living, but seem to have been made especially for the tomb (Figs. 154a, 154b).

Other types of Greek jewelry evolved and flourished with particular styles of clothing—and disappeared when these passed out of fashion. A case in point is the *fibula,* a cross between a brooch and a safety pin. Fibulas flourished throughout Greece until the sixth century B.C., after which they virtually passed out of existence (with the exception of Macedonia [Fig. 155], Etruria, and South Italy [Fig. 156], where they enjoyed a brief revival during the early Hellenistic Age).

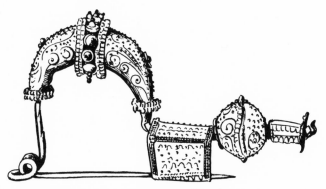

Fibula from South Italy, *Hamburg*

TECHNIQUE

The techniques employed in the creation of jewelry changed very little over the centuries until the advent of the Machine Age. Even today goldsmiths working in the bazaars of the Balkans and the Near and Middle East can be seen employing essentially the same methods used two thousand years ago.

Hammering, casting, cutting, joining, engraving, inlaying, and enameling were the chief techniques; sheet metal and wire, the basic raw materials. Sheet

178

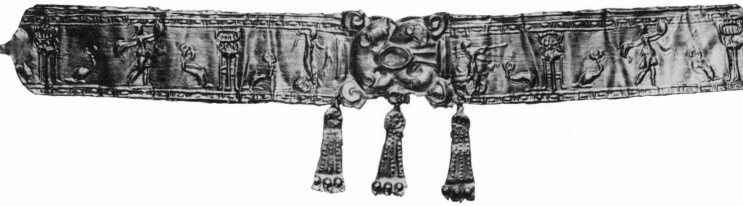

Fig. 154a. Funerary diadem with a "knot of Herakles," dancing maenads, tripods, and dolphins in relief. Later Hellenistic period, perhaps 1st century B.C. Leningrad Hermitage. Inv. no. 1838.45.
Museum photograph.

Fig. 154b. Funerary diadem decorated with embossed palmettes. Fourth-3rd centuries B.C. Musée des Beaux Arts, Budapest. Inv. no. 56.145A.
Museum photograph.

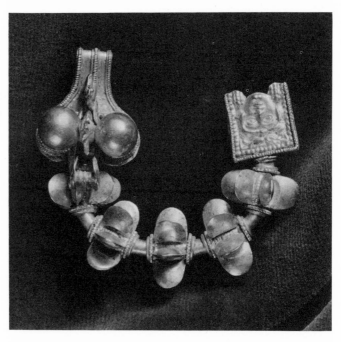

Fig. 155. "Millwheel" fibula. Northern Greek (Macedonian). Second half, 4th century B.C. Staatliche Museen, Berlin (West). Inv. no. 30219,42. *Photograph: Jutta Tietz-Glagow.*

Fig. 156. Pair of bow fibulas from Squinzano. Tarentine. Later 4th century B.C. Courtesy, Museum of Fine Arts, Boston. Acc. nos. 99.371, 99.372. H. L. Pierce Fund.

gold was made from bullion by hammering until the metal reached the desired thinness. (Today it is made by milling, but the convenient hand mill, now used by goldsmiths the world over, was at that time still unknown.) Next the metal would be rubbed or beaten into a mold or worked over a core. It could then be chased by using a hammer and a special tool. Stamping with a die-like puncheon was another technique that enjoyed great popularity, for it had the advantage of permitting the same ornament to be mechanically repeated many times. This technique was used especially for turning out the glittery ornaments that were sewn onto clothing.

The second basic raw material, wire, was most frequently made by twisting thin strips of sheet metal together and then rolling them between two plates of bronze or polished stone until they became round. In this way, wire acquired the slight—almost imperceptible—irregularities that are so pleasing to the eye.

Fine wire known as filigree was used for ornamental purposes. Special effects could be obtained by twisting the wire or by laying two countertwisted strands side by side so as to produce the appearance of braiding. Notched or "beaded" wires were also commonly employed. These decorative wires were welded in various patterns against a sheet-metal background by a special process that left no visible residue.

Much has been written about granulation in ancient jewelry. It was a technique known to the Minoans, Egyptians, Assyrians, Etruscans, and Greeks, and consisted basically of producing tiny pebbles, or granules, of gold and applying them to a surface as a form of decoration.

Until recently the process was a mystery. A few years ago, however, an English experimenter named Littledale finally succeeded in duplicating the technique. He mixed gold filings with powdered charcoal and subjected the mixture to a sufficiently high temperature to allow the filings to melt into tiny droplets (kept separate from each other by the charcoal). After cooling, the charcoal was washed away, leaving only the granules, which were sorted according to size by sifting through fine meshes.

Littledale's great problem was how to attach the tiny granules to their background, for there must be no visible evidence of a binding medium. In good ancient granulation, each grain is round and appears to be delicately poised on an absolutely smooth surface.

The secret of ancient granulation, as Littledale discovered, lay in the use of copper as a binding medium. Copper, when heated in conjunction with gold, brings the melting point of the two metals lower than that of either metal heated separately. He suspended a copper salt in thin glue brushed onto the surface to be granulated and arranged the granules in the desired pattern. When the piece of goldwork was heated, the glue vaporized and disappeared, and the copper salt—now converted to pure copper—alloyed itself with the surface of the gold, forming an invisible solder and leaving each granule still a perfect sphere. The result was a piece of granulation for all purposes indistinguishable from an ancient original.

PRECIOUS STONES

The striking effect produced by associating gold with precious stones first came to be appreciated in Greece during the early Hellenistic period, when Alexander's eastern conquests not only made available a wide variety of jewels but also opened Greece to many exotic influences. The red garnet and the green emerald were the preferred stones. They were polished rather than cut, so as to bring out their color instead of simply to reflect brilliant light. (Facet-cutting was a Roman innovation.) The transparent, glasslike rock crystal was popular for beads and pendants, as were sapphires and amethysts. Reddish-brown carnelian was most commonly used for inlays, beads, and pendants. Its warm color is pleasing against a tanned Mediterranean skin, and being relatively soft it can easily be carved into delicate shapes. The tiny doves that form the pendants of a pair of Hellenistic earrings in the Virginia Museum are examples of carnelian carving at its best (Fig. 157). Garnets were generally polished into round, oval, and heart-shaped beads, and were employed in the decorative pendants of earrings, diadems, and necklaces. Even the links of necklaces were sometimes carved of this stone (Fig. 158).

HISTORICAL SURVEY

Pre-Archaic and Archaic Periods

It is highly improbable that the collector of ancient art will ever come across Cycladic, Minoan, or Mycenaean jewelry, for it rarely appears on the market. There are few examples in private collections and a discussion of the earliest forms of classical jewelry will be dispensed with here.

Among the varieties of early Greek jewelry that do still find their way onto

Fig. 157. Dove earrings from Amphipolis. Fourth-3rd centuries B.C. Virginia Museum of Fine Arts, Richmond. *Photograph: Dietrich Widmer.*

Fig. 158. Gold and carnelian bandolier. Tarentine. Fourth-3rd centuries B.C. Swiss private collection. *Photograph: Hirmer, Munich.*

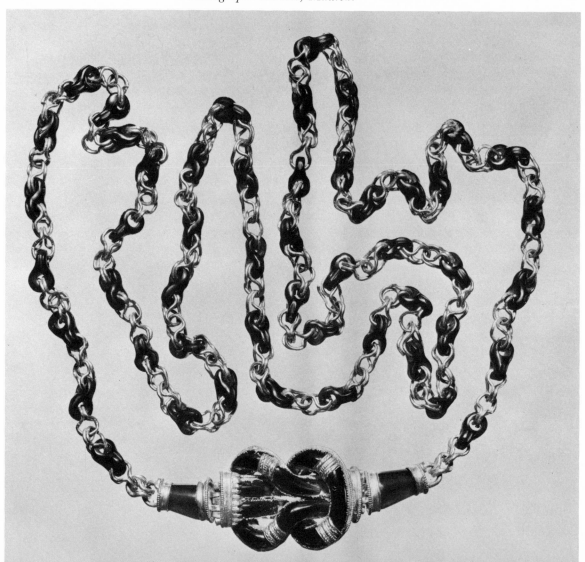

the art market are the funerary bands and diadems of the Geometric and Orientalizing periods. These consist of thin strips of gold or electrum (alloy of gold and silver), usually rounded at the ends and decorated with embossed or stamped designs featuring geometric ornaments, animals, and sometimes stylized human figures. Such objects were perhaps never worn by the living, for they are very thin and fragile, and their use may have been connected with funerary rites.

Less than a century after these relatively unsophisticated funerary bands, a more advanced type of jewelry began to develop in the eastern part of Greece and on the islands. Rhodes and western Asia Minor are the principal sources for the goldwork of the early Archaic period, in which the techniques of embossing and of granulation were frequently combined.

Archaic Rhodian plaque: Artemis as bee, *British Museum*

From Rhodes comes a rectangular electrum plaque with a large hook at the back for attachment (Fig. 159). A winged female holding two lions by their hind legs is shown. She is the Mistress of Wild Animals, a manifestation of the goddess Artemis frequently represented in Archaic art. Above the goddess, a lion head emerges from a rosette; below her are several small pomegranates, perhaps symbols of divinity. The edge of this tiny jewel, which is scarcely an inch and a half in height, is decorated with beaded and "strip twisted" wires. The ample use of granulation, both for indicating drapery patterns and for drawing the anatomical details of the figures themselves, is characteristic for this period, the second half of the seventh century B.C. Another superb piece of electrum jewelry from this age is a fibula, or garment clasp, in the shape of a bird of prey, believed to have been found in Asia Minor and recently acquired by the Berlin Museum (Fig. 160). It consists of a piece of foil beaten into the shape of a bird over a model or into a form. The edges have been bent back and "welded" to a plain base sheet. The head and body of the bird are decorated with fine granules that have been meticulously dropped into furrows.

During the seventh century the Greeks took over a variety of mythological monsters from their neighbors to the east, among them the sphinx and the griffin. The latter was thought to ward off evil, and human morals also came under his protection. An earring consisting of a thick gold wire bent into double fishhook shape and terminating at each end in a sculpted griffin head on a flat disk comes from the island of Melos (Fig. 161). This masterpiece of miniature sculpture seems to be filled with the same demonic power as the much larger caldron griffins discussed in the chapter on bronzes. (cf. p. 66).

Fig. 159. Rhodian plaque depicting the "Mistress of the Wild Beasts." Late 7th century B.C. Staatliche Museen, Berlin (West). Misc. Inv. no. 8943.
Photograph: Jutta Tietz-Glagow.

Fig. 161. Earring with griffin heads. From Melos. Seventh century B.C. Museum of Fine Arts, Boston. Acc. no. 99.378. H. L. Pierce Fund.
Museum photograph.

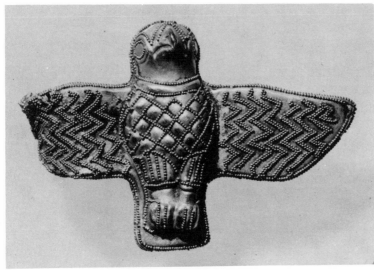

Fig. 160. Bird-shaped clasp. Electrum, finely granulated. Eastern Greek. Seventh century B.C. Staatliche Museen, Berlin (West). Inv. no. 1963.6.
Photograph: Jutta Tietz-Glagow.

Generally, Greek earrings of the seventh and sixth centuries B.C. are of simpler form, often consisting of nothing more elaborate than a simple spiral in one or several turns. A slim version of the omega sign, with the ends topped by a horizontal disk (often decorated with a rosette or a little tower of granulation), is fairly common. Another type, of which a fine example is in a Swiss private collection (Fig. 162), was worn looped over the ear rather than fastened to the lobe.

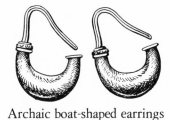

Archaic boat-shaped earrings

Archaic ear spirals, *Private Collection*

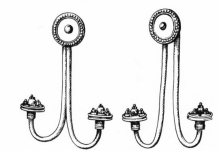

Archaic fishhook-shaped earrings, *Hamburg*

The Classical Period

Greek jewelry of the Classical period is very scarce. Gold, at this time, seems to have been reserved mainly for religious use.

The character of fifth-century Greek jewelry follows that of the Archaic period closely. Necklaces generally have large pendants, such as that in the form of a ram's head in the Berlin Museum (Fig. 163). Earrings tend to be large and elaborate, such as the pair with bees seated on multitiered rosettes, in Hamburg (Fig. 164). A similar motif is figured in the so-called "Capital Pin" of the Museum of Fine Arts, Boston (Fig. 165), a masterpiece of almost microscopic precision in which bees and lions are set in a maze of acanthus foliage atop an Ionic capital. By far the best examples of fifth-century jewelry come from South Russia and are exhibited in the Hermitage Museum of Leningrad. Both the Metropolitan Museum (New York) and the Museum of Fine Arts (Boston) do, however, possess outstanding collections of fifth-century Greek finger rings and ring stones.

Fifth-century bracelet, *Leningrad*

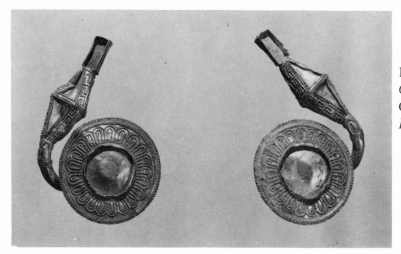

Fig. 162. Granulated earrings. Seventh-
6th centuries B.C. Kofler-Truniger
Collection, Lucerne.
Photograph: courtesy of the owner.

Fig. 163. Necklace with ram's-head
pendant. Late 6th century B.C. Staatliche Museen, Berlin (West). Inv. no.
misc. 8398.
Photograph: Jutta Tietz-Glagow.

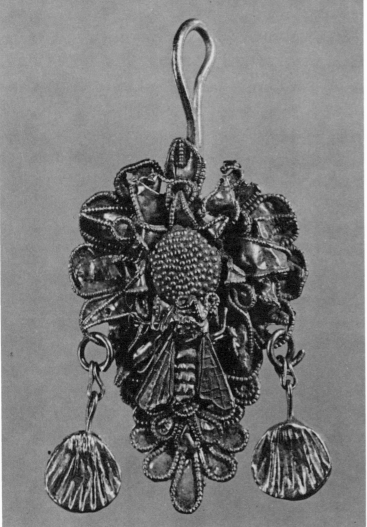

Fig. 164. An earring representing a bee seated on a palmette. From Ephesus. Eastern Greek. 5th century B.C. Museum für Kunst und Gewerbe, Hamburg. Inv. no. 1957, 54a-b St. 78-79. *Museum photograph.*

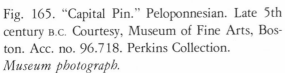

Fig. 165. "Capital Pin." Peloponnesian. Late 5th century B.C. Courtesy, Museum of Fine Arts, Boston. Acc. no. 96.718. Perkins Collection. *Museum photograph.*

Types of Hellenistic earrings, *Various Collections*

Hellenistic Period

In the latter part of the fourth century B.C., under the reign of Alexander the Great, Greece not only had recovered from the effects of the Persian Wars but had also succeeded in turning the tables on her Oriental oppressors. As the great cities of the Achaemenid East—Sardis, Susa, Persepolis—fell one by one in the path of Alexander's armies, vast riches began pouring into northern Greece. It was at this time that the wearing of jewelry once more came into popular fashion. Gold was plentiful again, rich sources having been discovered on Mount Pangaion in Macedonia.

The jewelry produced during this "golden" era—extending roughly from the thirties of the fourth century to the middle of the third—is undoubtedly the finest that the world has ever known. Virtually every type in vogue at this time was in some way influenced by the art of Achaemenid Iran. The heads of monsters and lions were a popular closure device for necklaces (Fig. 166) and even decorated finger rings (Fig. 167). Heads of ibex, the Persian animal par excellence, abound. Among the finest examples of ibex heads in Hellenistic jewelry are those on a pair of bracelets in a private collection (Fig. 168).

Another popular type is the armlet in the form of a snake, usually worn in pairs (Fig. 169). Such armlets consist of a massive gold band, rounded on

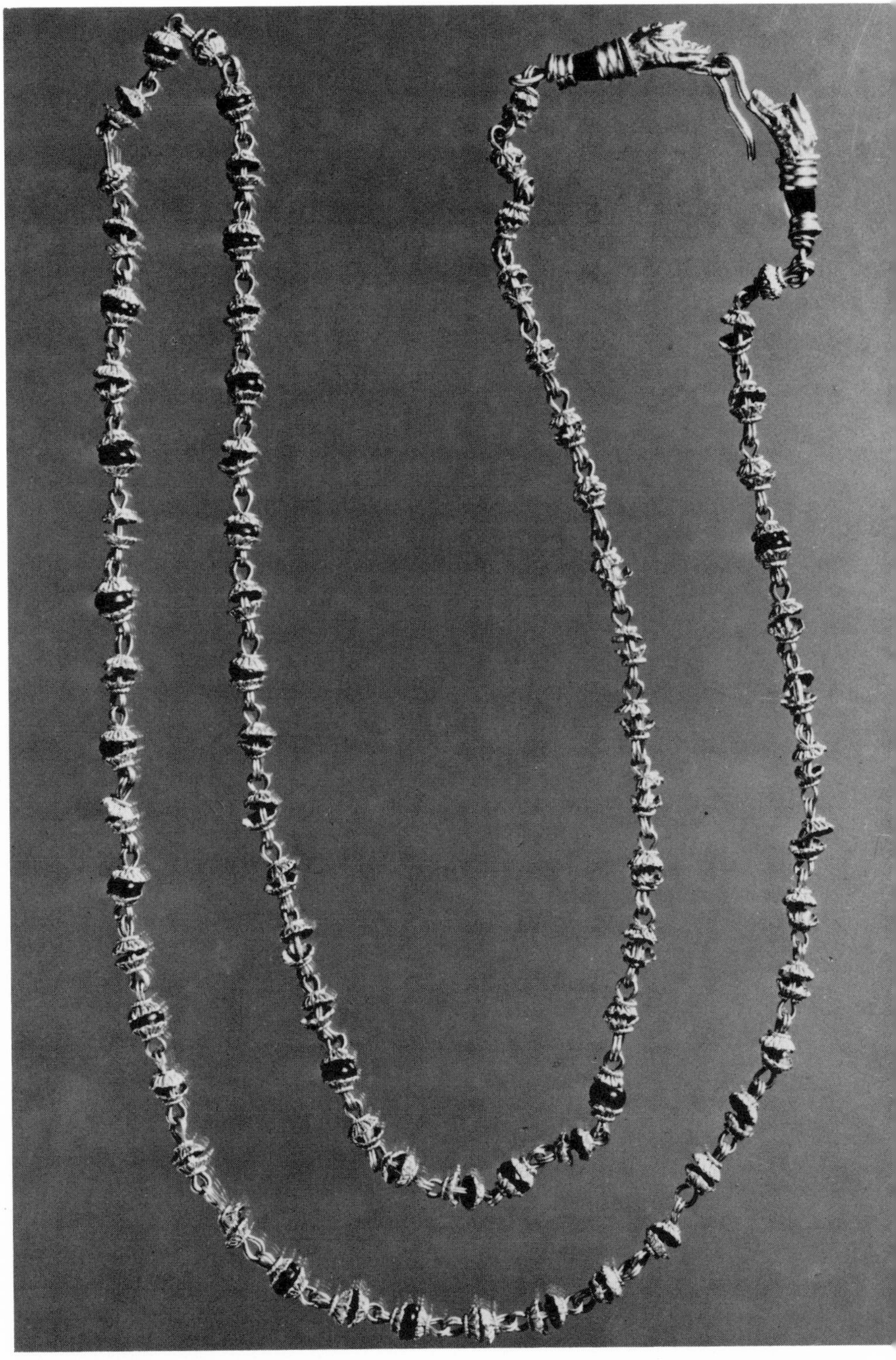

Fig. 166. Gold necklace with garnets
and dragon heads. Hellenistic, 3rd century B.C. Collection of the late Melvin
Gutman.
Photograph: courtesy of Allen Memor-
ial Art Museum, Oberlin College.

Fig. 167. Finger ring with lion heads.
Fourth - 3rd centuries B.C. Swiss private
collection.
Photograph: Hirmer, Munich.

Fig. 168. Antelope-head bracelets. Fourth - 3rd centuries B.C. Private collection.
Photograph: courtesy of the owner.

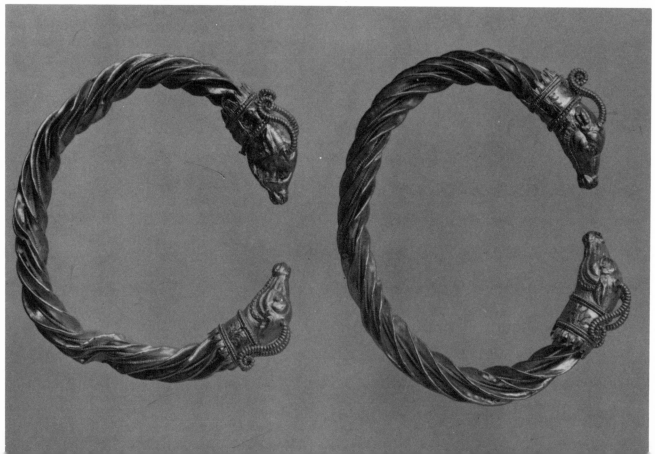

Fig. 169. Snake armlets. From South Italy. Fourth-3rd centuries B.C. Swiss private collection.
Photograph: Hirmer, Munich.

the outside and terminating in a finely sculptured head and forepart of a snake. The eyes and nostrils are generally worked with the hammer and puncheon, the scales with blows of the rounded chisel (Colorplate 20). An epigram by Antipater of Sidon, a poet of the second century B.C., tells us about a dedication made by five Athenian girls to the goddess Aphrodite. One of the objects described is "a beautifully coiled serpent, the golden adornment of her delicate limbs."

The wreaths of Olympian victors were made from boughs cut from sacred trees. Golden versions of such wreaths were dedicated to the gods in gratitude for victory at the games and were probably worn on special occasions. A number of fine gold wreaths of the Hellenistic period have come down to us virtually intact; they were almost certainly found in princely tombs. The leaves are represented in a very naturalistic manner, and sometimes blossoms and/or berries are represented as well. A typical example is the myrtle wreath from Amphipolis now in the Virginia Museum (Fig. 170).

The most common type of Hellenistic necklace consists of a flat strap plaited of many wires to one edge of which is affixed a row of "spearhead" or small "amphora" or bottle pendants (Fig. 171). The number of pendants varies from

Hellenistic strap necklace, *Hamburg*

Fig. 170. Myrtle wreath. Greek, from Amphipolis. Fourth-3rd centuries B.C. Virginia Museum of Fine Arts, Richmond.
Photograph: Dietrich Widmer.

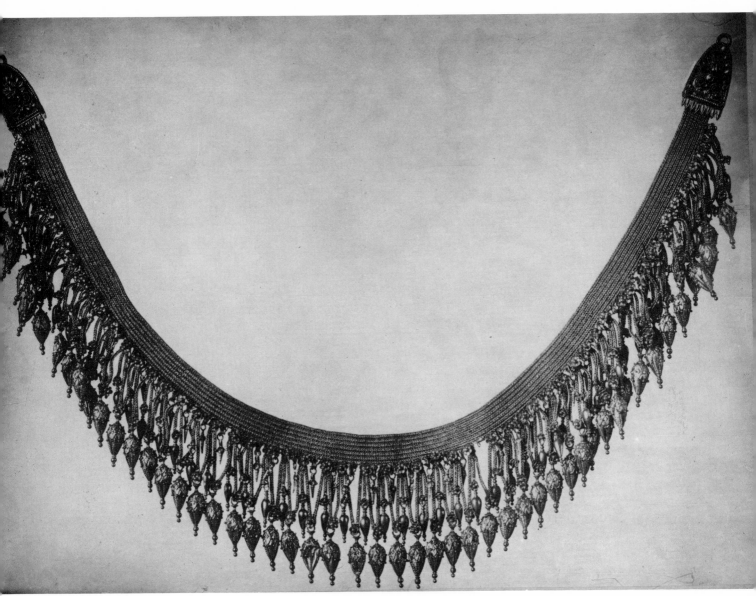

Fig. 171. Necklace with "amphora" pendants. Fourth century B.C. The Hermitage,
Leningrad.
Museum photograph.

twenty to over sixty. Such necklaces were generally pinned from shoulder to shoulder over a garment, rather than worn around the neck, and in this manner the pendants would dangle freely and be exhibited to maximum advantage. An inscription found by French excavators on the island of Delos mentions a necklace of this type hung with spearheads, dedicated in the local temple of Artemis by a certain courtesan named Simiche from the neighboring island of Mykonos. (Temple inventories from Delos also record the donation of necklaces with "amphora" pendants, the number of pendants on each necklace being dutifully recorded.) Other necklaces of the Hellenistic period consist of hollow gold beads alternating with beads of glass or semiprecious stone and ending in the heads of wild or domestic animals (Fig. 172).

Most plentiful of all the jewelry preserved from this brilliant epoch are the earrings. The finest example in existence is probably the "Nike Earring" in the Boston Museum (Fig. 173), a priceless jewel containing over a hundred separate parts.

Whereas the Boston earring is unique, related works do occasionally appear on the market. A fine earring with a pendant in the form of a Nike alighting recently entered the Virginia Museum (Fig. 174). A pair of Hellenistic earrings purchased by a Long Island collector represent Eros—the male counterpart of Nike (Fig. 175). A crouching Victory plays dice on the pyramidal cones of a

Hellenistic earrings, *Hamburg*

Fig. 172. Necklace with lynx-head terminals. Third century B.C. Swiss private collection.
Photograph: Hirmer, Munich.

Hellenistic pin, *Hamburg*

pair of earrings in Berlin (Fig. 176), while dolls and dancing girls dangle below on fine chains. Virtuosity of design combined with workmanship of high quality account for the extraordinary elegance of these ornaments.

Gold and silver pins decorated with tiny sculptures are a specialty of the Hellenistic Age that remained in vogue well into Roman times. On a gilt-silver example in Hamburg (Fig. 177), a standing Aphrodite combs her hair while a small Eros crouches on her shoulder. A pin in a South German private collection (Colorplate 21) is surmounted by a leafy Corinthian capital on which sits a crowned dove. The bird's feathers are formed of delicate filigree wires;

Fig. 173. Earring: Nike driving a chariot. Later 4th century B.C. Courtesy of the Museum of Fine Arts, Boston. Acc. no. 99.788. H. L. Pierce Fund. *Museum photograph.*

Fig. 174. Nike earring. Fourth-3rd centuries B.C. Virginia Museum of Fine Arts, Richmond.
Museum photograph.

198

Fig. 175. Eros earrings. Fourth-3rd
centuries B.C. Joseph Ternbach Collection, Great Neck, Long Island.
Photograph: courtesy of the owner.

Fig. 176. Earrings with Nike playing
dice. From Kalymnos. Ionian. Second
half, 4th century B.C. Staatliche Museen, Berlin (West). Inv. no. 30219,390.
Photograph: Jutta Tietz-Glagow.

Fig. 177. Aphrodite pin (detail). Alexandrian. Third-2nd centuries B.C. Museum für Kunst und Gewerbe, Hamburg. Inv. no. 1929,18.
Museum photograph.

Fig. 178. Thigh band with "Knot of Herakles" center-piece. Fourth-3rd centuries B.C. Christos Bastis Collection, New York.
Photograph: courtesy of the Brooklyn Museum.

the eyes contain enamel inlays, and the beak is a small cone of gold foil. An exquisite thigh band, now in the Bastis Collection, New York (Fig. 178), is a splendid example of the use of filigree during this period. It consists of a central "Herakles knot"—an ornamental reef knot to which certain magical properties were ascribed—richly overlaid with fine wire coils. To right and left the knot engages a pair of female heads to which the chain is fastened; lion heads form the terminal closures. The ornament was probably worn above the knee in the manner of a garter, and the effect on a shapely thigh must have been spectacular.

Hellenistic finger rings include a wide variety of types. Swivel rings were popular not only in Egypt and Syria, where they were set with scarabs, but throughout the Hellenistic world as well. A characteristic example (Fig. 179) shows the head and neck of a goddess with flamelike hair. A curious type of Hellenistic ring, believed to be of Alexandrian origin, is crowned by a veritable garden of granulation and filigree (Figs. 180a, 180b, 180c, 180d). The delicate ornaments, consisting of ivy leaves, tendrils, and berries, are protected by a thin plate of polished rock crystal. The effect surpasses the best efforts of Fabergé. A beautiful ring in the Museum of Fine Arts, Boston (Fig. 181) is composed of two intricately intertwined snakes—the royal animals of the Ptolemies—supporting a large emerald between them. It dates from the second to first centuries B.C. and is said to have been found in the Nile Delta.

The intaglio ring, with a picture gouged directly out of the round or oval gold bezel, remained in vogue from the Archaic through the Hellenistic periods (Figs. 182, 183).

Early Hellenistic finger rings

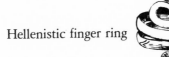

Hellenistic finger ring

Fig. 179. Swivel ring with head of a goddess. Gold and silver. South Italian. Fourth century B.C. Swiss private collection.
Photograph: Hirmer, Munich.

Figs. 180a, 180b, 180c, 180d. Ring with gold foliage and rock-crystal top. Fourth-3rd centuries B.C. Kofler-Truniger Collection, Lucerne.
Photograph: courtesy of the owner.

Fig. 181. Snake ring. Alexandrian. From Egypt. Second-
1st centuries B.C. Courtesy of the Museum of Fine Arts,
Boston. Edwin E. Jack Fund.
Museum photograph.

Fig. 182. Intaglio ring, figuring a rooster and a mouse.
Elektron. Late 6th century B.C. Museum für Kunst und
Gewerbe, Hamburg. Inv. no. 1967,4.
Museum photograph.

Fig. 183. Intaglio-cut finger ring figuring a female bust
in profile. From South Italy. Hellenistic. Formerly on the
Roman art market.
*Photograph: courtesy of the German Archaeological In-
stitute, Rome.*

SELECT BIBLIOGRAPHY

C. Alexander, *The Art of the Goldsmith in Classical Times* (New York: Metropolitan Museum of Art, 1928). Short descriptive guide to the Metropolitan's excellent collection of ancient jewelry; out of print.

P. Amandry, *Collection Hélène Stathatos. Les Bijoux antiques* (Strasbourg, Vol. I, Vol. II, 1953; Vol. III, 1963). Scholarly catalog of one of the leading collections of Greek jewelry.

R. A. Higgins, *Greek and Roman Jewellery* (London: Methuen, 1961). Useful general survey arranged chronologically and by types. Well indexed, with bibliography and list of sites for those intending to pursue the study of jewelry further.

H. Hoffmann and P. F. Davidson, *Greek Gold: Jewelry from the Age of Alexander* (New York: Brooklyn Museum of Art, 1965). Catalog of the recent international exhibition of Hellenistic jewelry, with an important introductory section on technique.

F. H. Marshall, *Catalogue of the Jewellery . . . in the British Museum* (London, 1911). Most types of Greek, Roman, and Etruscan jewelry are included in the heliogravure plates of this exemplary catalog of the world's largest and most important jewelry collection. Out of print.

6

Coins

by Herbert A. Cahn

The English numismatist and archaeologist Percy Gardner once described the study of Greek coins as "the grammar of Greek art." Pick up three Greek coins— a Corinthian stater of the sixth century B.C. (Fig. 184), a four-drachma piece of Syracuse dating from the height of the Classical period (Fig. 185), and a te- tradrachm of Alexander the Great minted in Alexandria (Fig. 186)—and take a closer look. Gardner's words immediately take on meaning. The three main phases of Greek art represented in originals of high quality lie in the palm of our hand. The Corinthian Athena head conforms to the contours of the coin; the features lack interrelation. Only a flashing eye and the hint of a smile betray the inner life of this early masterpiece of the engraver's art. Now compare the head of the nymph Arethusa surrounded by four dolphins on the Syracusan coin minted only one hundred years later. But what a long way the die cutter's art—and art in general—has come in this short space of time! The transitions from the stylized coiffure to the features of the face, from mouth to cheek, from chin to neck, are exquisitely modeled, and the whole surface of the coin pul- sates with animation. Take, finally, the Herakles head on the coin of Alexan- der dating from around 325 B.C. Another immense stride. Dynamic pathos now keynotes the features of this head, in which contemporaries recognized the por-

The coins illustrated in Figures 184-186, and on plates I-III belong to a Swiss private collector. Figures 184-186 are enlarged. The others are reproduced to scale (photographs by H. A. Cahn).

Fig. 184. Corinth. Silver stater ca. 550 B.C. Obverse: flying Pegasus. Reverse: head of the goddess Athena.

Fig. 185. Syracuse. Tetradrachm ca. 450 B.C. Obverse: victorious chariot; the goddess Nike crowning the horses. Reverse: head of the fountain-nymph Arethusa surrounded by four dolphins and the name of the city ("Syrakosion").

Fig. 186. Alexander the Great. Tetradrachm, struck at Alexandria (Egypt, ca. 325 B.C.) Obverse: head of Heracles in a lion-skin, with the traits of Alexander. Reverse: Zeus seated holding scepter and eagle. To right, the name ("Alexandrou"). To left, rose (moneyer's symbol). Under the chair, name of magistrate ("Dio . . .").

trait of Alexander. The world ruler has appropriated the attributes of the hero Herakles on this coin.

We have simply selected three random examples from a wealth of existing material, examples such as may still be easily acquired at relatively low cost from any established coin dealer. In contrast to many other classes of Greek art, Greek coins, owing to the durability of their precious metal and to the fact that they were hoarded in antiquity, have come down to us in immense numbers. So plentiful, in fact, are the preserved examples that we are able to survey the entire development of Greek numismatic art in a virtually unbroken sequence. In other words, the claim that Greek coins can be considered a basic grammar of Greek art is amply justified.

One objection to coin collecting that might be raised cannot be lightly discarded: How can such small objects be accorded the same interest as works of monumental art, for example, temples, statues, and even vases? Admittedly, the appreciation of coins as works of art is difficult at first, for our eye does not adapt itself readily to their small scale. We overcome this hurdle by looking at coins with a powerful magnifying glass and illustrating them considerably enlarged. The very fact that they in no way suffer from magnification is the ultimate proof of the die cutter's monumental outlook and truly creative élan.

Of course, the Greek coin was not intended to be admired under magnification. In ancient Greece a work of art was appreciated according to its quality and not its size. Theodoros of Samos, who was active during the reign of the tyrant Polycrates (circa 535-522 B.C.), built temples, invented the art of hollow-casting metal, wrote books on architecture, and carved the ring of Polycrates. We know that Phidias was a goldsmith. So highly did the Sicilians esteem their die engravers that the most famous of these masters were accorded the privilege of signing their works.

Another reason why Greek coins are of such inestimable importance is that they are official documents of state. The Greek coin embodies the pictorial essence of the *polis*, the Greek city-state. And since the Greeks considered the images and attributes of their gods to be the very embodiments of statehood, their coins are a vital source of information regarding the prime cults of any given polis. The head of a divinity on a coin guaranteed the correct alloy and weight, for the standard of weights and measures was sacred.

The coinage of our day is lacking in inspiration. It employs hackneyed sym-

bols, and can at best be considered as an example of routine, if technically perfect, academism. Official art today is rarely avant-garde. Not so in ancient
Greece. Coin series, such as those of Syracuse and Kyzikos, clearly demonstrate
that the state merely prescribed the subject of the coin representation and that the
die cutter was left a free hand in the interpretation and execution of the theme.
With this high degree of independence allowed, artists rivaled one another in
the originality and daring of their designs.

The study of Greek coinage presents many fascinating aspects. Apart from
the artistic and religious viewpoint already described, Greek coins provide important documents for the economic and political history of Greece. The Athenian attempt to monopolize world trade during the fifth century, the rise of Philip
of Macedon and of his son Alexander, the contacts of Greece with her eastern
neighbors, the penetration of Greek culture and Greek trade into the remot-
est corners of the Mediterranean world (including Gaul, the Balkans, and even
Southern Russia)—all these events of world history can be clearly traced through
coinage.

HOW WERE GREEK COINS MADE?

Greek coins were made mainly of three metals: gold, silver, and bronze. The
earliest Greek coins are of "electrum," a natural alloy consisting of approximately
two-thirds gold and one-third silver. Pure gold was also used for coins from
the middle of the sixth century B.C., but the metal was only minted sporadic-
ally up to the time of Philip II of Macedon (reigned, 359-336 B.C.) (Plate III, 6).
The principal metal for Greek coinage was silver. Bronze had been used for
small change since the late fifth century. The most important silver mines were
those of Spain and northern Greece, although Athens had its own mine at Lau-
rion on the eastern coast of Attica, not far from Cape Sounion. In fact, this mine
is still operating today.

With few exceptions (cast bronze coins of Sicily and Olbia-Odessa), Greek
coins are *struck*. That is to say, the relief on each side of the coin is produced
by the mechanical pressure of two dies. The ancient minting process was approximately as follows:

Preparation of the Metal

The bullion (in the form of bars) was cut into small pieces, the weight of which
corresponded to the weight of the coin to be produced. These pieces were then

cast into spherical shape (flans). Sometimes the bullion was melted directly, and the flans were produced by casting into standardized molds.

Preparation of the Die

The coin die is a wedge-shaped or cylindrical tool of bronze or tempered iron. After the surface of this tool was polished smooth, the design was engraved with a cutting tool (burin). Hubs were used for the letters of the inscription and sometimes for certain details of the coin type. The die cutter's technique derives directly from the ancient tradition of gem cutting, which had flourished in Greece since the early second millennium B.C. It is generally believed that Greek die cutters also engaged in the engraving of gems and precious metals.

The Minting Process

The obverse die, with its slightly concave surface, was set into a depression in the anvil. The flan was laid over this obverse die, and the reverse die was placed on top of it (see drawing). The reverse die had a slightly convex surface and therefore exerted the greater pressure when struck. The minter held the flan and the reverse die in place with tongs, and struck the latter with a hammer. The intaglio-cut designs of the two dies were thereby transferred to the obverse and reverse of the coin, where they appear in relief. In cases where a very high relief was desired, some form of mechanical die punch—probably a drop hammer operated by animal power—must have been employed. The flan was never heated (as we are erroneously informed in a number of handbooks) but was always struck cold.

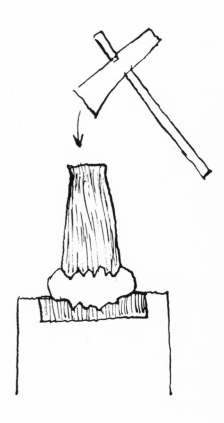

The minting process has remained basically unchanged over the ages. Only the cutting of the die and the striking of the flan have been mechanized to a considerable extent. The ancient handmade coins, often carelessly produced, frequently reveal flaws: rims burst through excess pressure, improperly centered designs (cf. Plate II, 12), marks left by rusty or cracked dies (cf. Plate I, 8). Such imperfections actually enhance the charm of the coin. No two Greek coins, even those minted at the same time, are exactly alike.

No description of the actual operation of a Greek mint has come down to us. We do know from Roman sources, however, that the Roman state mint was a vast and highly organized undertaking involving a complicated division of labor. A Greek mint cannot have been so very different. Considering the number of coins produced by nearly every city, it must have teemed with people: overseers controlling every step in production, metal testers, die cutters, weight controllers, and slaves for all the menial tasks.

VALUES AND CURRENCIES

Before we proceed to sketch the history of Greek coinage, we must say a word about the basic arithmetic involved:

1 talent = 60 mines	gold : electrum : silver = 13⅓ : 10 : 1
1 mine = 100 drachmas	silver : bronze = 1 : 120
1 drachma = 6 obols	(these proportions are apt to vary)

This simple system is the basis of all Greek coinage. The two large denominations, talent and mine, were units of weight rather than coins (the large gold minae of the Ptolemies, weighing 28 grams, form an exception). One paid for a mine with one hundred drachm pieces, or twenty-five tetradrachms. The mine—both as a fiscal concept and as a standard of weight—derives from the ancient Near East. The word "drachma" means "a handful" in Greek: the human hand is able to grasp six iron spits, or *obeloi.* Iron spits were a primitive form of currency before the invention of coinage. Spits of this sort were found in great number in the sanctuary of Hera at Argos. They were obviously used only as money, and no longer served any practical purpose. The name of the smallest denomination of Greek coinage—*obolos*—derives from these spits.

Here are the other units of Greek coinage:

Hemidrachmon or triobolon	=	½ drachma (3 obols)
Didrachmon	=	2 drachmas
Tridrachmon	=	3 drachmas
Tetradrachmon or tetrachmon	=	4 drachmas, the most common large denomination of silver-coinage
Oktadrachmon	=	8 drachmas
Dekadrachmon	=	10 drachmas; these are rare "dollar-sized" coins; they were minted for special occasions only.
Tetartemorion	=	¼ obol, one of the smallest coins: weight 0.2 g.

Hemiobolon	=	½ obol
Tritartemorion	=	¾ obol
Trihemiobolon	=	1½ obols
Diobolon	=	2 obols
Triobolon or Hemidrachmon	=	3 obols
Tetrobolon	=	4 obols

We frequently find the "stater" mentioned in Greek literature. The word signifies "established unit," and refers to any monetary unit larger than a drachma. In literary sources and in inscriptions, it is generally accompanied by the location of the mint or the name of the ruler. Thus, for example, "Kyzikenos" refers to the large electrum staters of Kyzikos, and "Philippeios" to the gold staters of Philip of Macedon (cf. Plate III, 6).

Ancient Greece never possessed a unified monetary system. From the very beginning several standards co-existed, most of them deriving from ancient Near Eastern weight standards that were established long before the invention of coins.

Not until the beginning of the Classical period did several main currencies emerge. To name the most important: the Attic-Euboean, with a drachma of circa 4.3 grams; the Aeginetan, with a drachma of circa 6.2 grams (called a "heavy drachma" in antiquity); and the Phocaean.

A word must be said about monetary transactions in antiquity. A Greek money changer would accept a great variety of well-known coins as species (for example, the "owl" of Athens, the "pegasos" of Corinth, the "turtle" of Aegina, and so on). Those not familiar to him he would weigh on his scales. A peasant from Megara wanting to change his Corinthian staters for Athenian currency might be required to add an obol to each two staters in order to receive a full Attic tetradrachm. One can conjure up the animated discussions, accompanied by eloquent gestures, that must have been part of such a transaction.

HISTORIC SURVEY

The Forerunners

Many different forms of payment for goods received were in use before the invention of coinage. We are familiar with them from actual surviving documents

used as money, from pictorial representations, and from literary sources such as the Old Testament. Primitive forms of payment included barter with cattle, beads, and utilitarian objects. When in the Bible (Genesis 24:22) one reads of Isaac giving his wife Rebekah "a golden earring of half a shekel weight, and two bracelets of ten shekels weight of gold for her hand," it is clear that a more sophisticated unit of value has been attained: precious metal of standarized form and set weight. Other types of pre-coinage currency include copper ingots, such as those found in great number in Crete and Cyprus as well as in shipwrecks of the Late Bronze Age, utilitarian objects such as the spits *(obeloi)* mentioned above, raw ore of various sizes and shape, and finally, drop-shaped money of electrum and silver, cast in units the weights of which were continued in a later age in coinage. Drop-shaped money has been found at various sites in Asia Minor and Crete.

The Earliest Coins

The step from these metal slugs to the invention of actual coinage was a relatively small one. Simply by providing one of these slugs of precious metal with a stamp indicating an official guarantee of value, the coin was born: "a handy piece of metal issued by the state, guaranteeing a certain weight and content by virtue of picture and/or inscription."

The ancients attributed the invention of coinage to the Lydians who inhabited western Asia Minor during the first half of the first millennium B.C. Gyges, Alyattes, and Croesus were the most famous Lydian kings, and the name Alyattes (607? - 560 B.C.) is thought by some scholars to occur on an early electrum coin. The very first coins—even earlier than those of Alyattes—were primitive Lydian coins of electrum, bearing a rectangular stamp on the reverse and a strip design on the front. They date from the second half of the seventh century B.C.; some were found in the Ephesian Artemision. Although apparently Lydian, these coins also circulated in the Greek coastal cities, where they seem to have been imitated (see marginal drawings). Such primitive coinage soon became unsatisfactory to the Greeks, who seized upon the coin as a vehicle for artistic expression. Very soon, the obverses of these early electrum coins were enlivened with pictures of great variety. The simple utilitarian object was thus transformed into a work of art.

Along the coast of Asia Minor, in the ancient Greek centers of Miletus, Ephesus, and Smyrna—cities that had witnessed the birth of Greek philosophy—

originated the oldest electrum currencies. These early coins were minted down
to the smallest denominations (1/96 of a stater). Only the obverse was decorated
with a relief. The reverse received the so-called "incuse square," a small rectangular depression, for the reverse side of the coin was struck with the upper
(convex) half of the die, which held the flan in place on the anvil by means of
a square sharp-edged projection at the center (cf. Plate I, 6).

Once invented, coinage spread rapidly. Greece proper was poor in gold
but rich in silver, and it is not surprising that this is where the earliest silver
issues are found (in Naxos, Paros, Siphnos, and especially in Aegina, the flourishing emporium in the Saronic Gulf) (cf. Plate I, 1). The silver staters of the
Aegean islands, particularly the "turtles" of Aegina, were the Greek motherland's answer to the electrum currency of the Ionian East.

Aristotle reports that Solon put through a currency reform in the year
593 B.C. in which he "enlarged the coins." This is taken to refer to the Athenian tetradrachmas with the head of Athena and the owl, the earliest group of
which can be dated stylistically to about 590 B.C. Prior to these coins the Athenians had been issuing a silver stater on the Aeginetan standard, featuring an
amphora of a shape current around 600 B.C.

Shortly thereafter coins were being minted throughout the entire Greek
world. Besides the principal issues, such as those of Corinth, Aegina, Athens,
Thasos, Miletus, and Syracuse, innumerable other cities issued coins for their
own needs as well as those of the surrounding countryside. A great variety of
standards arose. In addition to the gold standard of Persia and the electrum standard of Asia Minor, silver became the main metal for minting. The subdivision
of denominations even down to fractions of the obol shows that there were coins
even for the humblest needs and that everyone participated in the money-based
economy. Whereas some cities, like Athens, Corinth, and Aegina, adhered to
one type of coin which circulated all over the Mediterranean, others, like Kyzikos, Cyrene, and Syracuse, issued a great variety of types. The early coinage
of peripheral regions, like South Italy, Sicily, northern Greece, and the Cyrenaica, was of surprisingly high quality. The techniques also attained a very high
standard during this early period: the metal of the dies was tempered for greater
durability; the art of striking both sides of the coin with a high relief was developed. The most popular subjects were city emblems, the animal-shaped attributes of divinities, and the divinities themselves (sometimes the head alone,
sometimes the whole figure).

The pictorial repertoire of Archaic Greek coins shows the greatest variety. A satyr is represented carrying off a nymph (cf. Plate I, 3). Lions are shown attacking bulls and wild boars. The winged Nike sails through the air, gracefully lifting a fold of her drapery. A luscious bunch of grapes is shown, as are four fiery horses drawing a quadriga. Pallas Athena and her owl stare forth at the beholder from another coin (cf. Plate I, 2). On yet another, Poseidon, a superior smile playing on his lip, wields his trident against the giants.

During the fifth century the art of coinage spread far and wide throughout Mediterranean lands. Bronze now began to be used, and gradually usurped silver for minting small change (cf. Plate II, 11; Plate III, 5). The great event in the history of Greek art—the transition from Archaic to Classical art shortly after 500 B.C.—was promoted by the die cutter just as strongly as by the vase painter, the sculptor, and the architect. The transformation can be observed most clearly in the great coin series of Syracuse, Corinth, Kyzikos, and Knidos. The innovators often had to struggle against the traditionalists. There was often a tendency to continue Archaic pictorial traditions, especially in the coinage of Athens and Aegina, for it had been circulated to all corners of the world and Greeks and barbarians alike had grown accustomed to it. This explains why the most original designs are those developed in the peripheral mints. The coinage produced during the fifth century in places like northern Greece, Asia Minor, and especially Sicily, far surpasses anything produced in the motherland during the same period, in quality and invention.

The heads of divinities on coins of the Early Classical Age express supreme nobility. The Apollo of Catane, the Dionysos of Naxos, and the Hermes of Ainos are of unequaled majesty. Bodies become lithe; eyes mirror the soul.

By the middle of the fifth century Athens had achieved a monopoly over coinage throughout its empire. A decree signed by Klearchos (449-448 B.C.) forbade the allies of Athens either to mint their own coins or to accept non-Attic currencies in payment. This historical fact is borne out by the numismatic evidence: Whereas between the years 450-430 B.C. no coins appear to have been struck in the cities of the Athenian empire other than Athens, the issue of Athenian "owls" during these years shows a marked increase. In Sicily an unrivaled explosion of talent occurred about 430 B.C. It seems to have lasted for an entire generation. Die cutters now became keenly aware of their role as creative artists. Some of them—for example, Euainetos (cf. Plate III, 1), Kimon, and Herakleidas—affixed their signatures for all posterity. Their creations, in daringly high relief, defy the limitations imposed by the size and the technical possibilities of coinage.

Other artists produced animal portraits of great virtuosity that truly capture the very essence of the animal represented—the eagles and the crabs of Akragas, the hares of Messana, the swans of Camarina. Some cities departed from the traditional types. Kyzikos, Mytilene, and Abdera, for example, changed their coin designs each year (whereas Tarentum, Ainos, and Syracuse preferred frequent variations on a traditional theme).

During the fourth century B.C., and later, widespread use was made of copper for small change. The standards of size and weight were no longer so stringently adhered to for these small denominations. This is the final period during which the die cutter could still give full rein to his imagination; the finest works of fourth-century B.C. numismatic art are to be found in the coinage of South Italy, northern Greece, the Peloponnese, Crete, and Asia Minor. Philip and Alexander of Macedon monopolized Greek coinage now—with even more spectacular success than had the Athenians in the preceding period. The coins of Alexander circulated from Pella to Babylon and Alexandria during the ruler's lifetime, to the virtual exclusion of all other coinage.

Royal portraits keynote the development of coinage during the Hellenistic period (cf. Plate III, 7 - 10). Kingdoms large and small represented their rulers on their coins. Only the Ptolemies in Egypt and the Attalids in Pergamon were content with restricting coin portraiture to the founders of their dynasties. Far to the east, in Bactria and in India, the coinage of the local dynasts maintained a Greek character for centuries. The same applies for the various regions that the Romans never conquered, as well as those regions that for various reasons were able to maintain a certain autonomy under Roman rule (for example, Thessaly, Aetolia, Achaea).

COLLECTING COINS

Not infrequently a seemingly insignificant experience may inspire a person to become a keen collector of coins. A philatelist notices a drachma of Alexander the Great priced at twenty dollars in the showcase of his stamp dealer, buys it and, along with it, a handbook on Greek coins. At home he reads up on his acquisition and learns about works of art that seemed hitherto beyond his reach. He gives up stamp collecting and becomes a numismatist. While unable to afford top-quality pieces, he nevertheless succeeds, within a relatively short time, in assembling a small collection of Greek coins in which every historical period is represented in one or more well-preserved examples.

A tourist picks up a Greek silver coin as a souvenir of his visit to Athens, Istanbul, or Taormina. Amazingly, it turns out not to be a modern forgery (such as are offered to tourists by the thousands) but, as he is informed by an expert, a Greek original of the fourth century B.C. He soon learns that a similar coin in better condition could have been acquired for the same price at home.

The coin-collecting passion has taken hold of both these gentlemen. Both have learned that collecting coins is not only a joy to the eye but also a way of deepening their knowledge and making history come to life. How often do they find themselves musing idly over questions that can never be answered: Through whose hands has this coin passed? For what was it given in payment? Why did its last owner commit it to the soil? Such silent dialogues are among the greatest pleasures of the amateur who builds his collection, not for reasons of prestige or investment, but for his own personal fulfillment.

HOW TO DISPLAY AND CARE FOR COINS

I am an advocate of the old-fashioned opinion that coins should be kept in trays rather than in closed containers or in plastic envelopes. Coins should be picked up, turned over, handled; they should be laid out in rows in a meaningful and easily visible arrangement. For small collections there exist small portable chests containing a number of drawers lined with cloth or leather each divided into many compartments. For the larger collection the coin cabinet is still the best solution. The coins lie in compartmented drawers, and the entire cabinet can be built into a safe. Metal drawers are not to be recommended, since the magnetic field they set up, however slight, is apt to cause surface deterioration, especially of silver coins. Mahogany coin cabinets with smooth-sliding drawers are manufactured in England. They can accommodate large numbers of coins. The entire British Museum coin collection is stored in such cabinets.

Keeping a card file or a catalog of one's coin collection is time-consuming but highly recommended. Describing and classifying coins is the best way to broaden one's knowledge about them. In fact, it is more than apt to lead to independent scholarly research. Ideally, a catalog file should be accompanied by photographs of each coin. A coin collector in Seattle, Washington, Norman Davis, has recently published his Greek coins.* His book is a model collector publication.

If the collector has no time to keep a catalog, he should at least place a ticket giving the essential data under each coin. For example:

*Greek Coins and Cities, 1967.

Sicily	verso	purchased from . . .
Akragas		
Didrachmon		
ca. 470 b.c.		Paris, May 1965
AKPA Eagle to 1.		($36)
Rev. crab		
BMC 11		

A word about cleaning coins. Very often the peasant who finds an ancient coin hoard will scrub the oxidized coins until their metal shines. Most coins are ruined by this drastic procedure. Unfortunately, even educated coin collectors frequently ruin their coins in exactly the same manner. The amateurish use of mechanical or chemical cleaning procedures is to be avoided at all costs. Dry brushing (never with nylon bristles!) or washing with soap and water will generally suffice to remove loose dirt. More complicated cleaning procedures, such as electrolysis or chemical treatment, should be left to the specialist who has been trained to caution by long experience.

Where Can Greek Coins Be Obtained?

Any respectable coin dealer is able to offer a selection of Greek coins at reasonable prices and to guarantee the authenticity of each coin sold. By "respectable" I mean those dealers affiliated with the International Association of Professional Numismatists* (IAPN). All members are bound fully to guarantee the authenticity of the coins they sell; many will also provide detailed numismatic information. (Unfortunately, there are very few dealers specialized in Greek numismatics in the United States.) A number of coin dealers issue illustrated price lists, which they generally distribute free of charge, on request. The same applies also to the richly illustrated and, in many instances, conscientiously edited auction-sale catalogs that appear periodically. When acquiring coins at auctions, one should naturally give preference to firms that offer guarantees of authenticity.

A word of warning must finally be sounded concerning the acquisition of coins at bargain prices in their lands of origin, such as Italy, Greece, Turkey, Lebanon, and Egypt. Among the authentic material lurks many a spurious coin,

*Membership lists are available from the Secretary (D. J. Crowther, 76 New Bond St., London W. 1) or from the American Vice-President of the Association (H. Christensen, Hudson County National Bank Building, 95 River Street, Hoboken, New Jersey).

and it is particularly the spectacular pieces that are most likely to be fakes. Their detection is sometimes no easy matter, even for the specialist.

PUBLIC COIN COLLECTIONS

One day the collector of Greek coins will pluck up his courage and knock on the closed door of a museum coin room in order to seek information and advice and to compare his pieces with those in a public collection. He should not let himself be discouraged by the treasures encountered there. These collections grew over generations, at an enormous investment of public and private funds, and were frequently enriched by donations of entire private collections. The more important public coin collections are administered by trained numismatists who will be glad to assist the collector with their specialized knowledge. In most cases the numismatic library attached to the departmental collection can be consulted on application.

To name a few important collections:

The American Numismatic Society in *New York* is an institution unique in the world in that it combines a research center with a superb collection, particularly of Greek coins (Audubon Terrace, Broadway between 155th and 156th streets). The Museum of Fine Arts, *Boston,* possesses a magnificent collection of Greek coins, with the emphasis on artistic quality. Mention might also be made of the university collections in *St. Louis* (Washington University) and *Cambridge* (Harvard University, Fogg Art Museum).

In England the leading collection is naturally that of the British Museum in *London* (Department of Coins and Medals), which has published its holdings in a series of exemplary catalogs. The university collections of *Oxford* and *Cambridge,* and the Hunterian Museum in *Glasgow* are also of high standing.

On the Continent the most important coin collections are to be found in *Paris* (Cabinet des Médailles), *East Berlin, Leningrad* (Hermitage), and *Athens* (National Museum); *Copenhagen* (National Museum), *Munich* (Staatliche Münzsammlung), *Brussels* (Bibliothèque royale), *The Hague* (Royal Coin Cabinet), *Istanbul,* and *Vienna* (Kunsthistorisches Museum); *Milan* (Castello Sforzesco), the *Vatican,* and the National Museums of *Florence, Naples, Palermo,* and *Syracuse.* The Italian and Greek coin collections are not normally open to the public; obtaining authorization to visit them may be difficult.

In conclusion, I should like to express my sincere thanks to the Swiss collector who permitted me to photograph the Greek coins reproduced in the illustrations. Many of them are published for the first time.

Plate I

Archaic Greek Coins

1 Island of Aegina. Early silver stater. Ca. 600 B.C.
Obverse: turtle. Reverse: incuse square.

2 Athens. Silver tetradrachm. Ca. 540 B.C.
Obverse: helmeted head of the goddess Athena. Reverse: owl and olive twig.

3 Uncertain mint of Macedon or Thrace. Silver stater. Ca. 520 B.C.
Obverse: satyr and nymph. Reverse: incuse square.

4 Klazomenai, Ionia. Silver stater. Ca. 520 B.C.
Obverse: forepart of winged boar. Reverse: incuse square.

5 Erythrai, Ionia. Silver stater. Ca. 520 B.C.
Obverse: youthful horseman. Reverse: incuse square.

6 Kyzikos, on the south shore of the Propontis. Electrum one-sixth of stater. Ca. 500 B.C.
Obverse: helmeted head of Athena. Reverse: incuse square.

7 Knidos, Karia. Silver drachma. Ca. 510 B.C.
Obverse: forepart of lion. Reverse: head of the goddess
Aphrodite in incuse square.

8 Island of Kos in the Dodecanese. Silver three-sikloi piece.
Ca. 480 B.C.
Obverse: discus thrower and tripod; city name "Koion."
Reverse: crab in incuse square.

9 Syracuse. Silver didrachmon about 490 B.C.
Obverse: bearded horseman. Reverse: head of Arethusa
surrounded by three dolphins and the name of the city
(see Fig. 185).

10 Kaulonia in southern Italy. Silver nommos ca. 520 B.C.
Obverse: standing Apollo (kouros type), in the right
hand a twig, on his left arm the figure of a running man
carrying a twig. In front, stag; behind, city name "Kaul"
Probably the illustration of a local lustration rite. Reverse: same type incuse.

11 Kroton in southern Italy. Silver nommos, ca. 530 B.C.
Obverse: tripod, city name "Kro." Between the legs of
the tripod are two snakes. Reverse: incuse tripod.

12 Metapontion in southern Italy. Silver nommos, ca. 510 B.C.

Plate II

Classical Greek Coins

1 Athens. Silver tetradrachm, ca. 440 B.C. of similar type as Plate I, 2, but of later style.

2 Athens. Silver didrachmon, ca. 480 B.C. Similar.

3 Athens. Silver drachm, ca. 480 B.C. Similar.

4 Athens. Silver obol, ca. 350 B.C. Similar.

5 Ainos, Thrace. Silver tetradrachm, ca. 460 B.C.
Obverse: head of the god Hermes. Reverse: city name "Aini"; goat and amphora in incuse square.

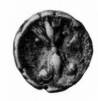

6 Elis near Olympia. Silver stater ca. 380 B.C.
Obverse: head of Zeus's eagle. Reverse: thunderbolt.

7 Elis near Olympia. Silver stater ca. 370 B.C.
Obverse: head of Zeus. Reverse: eagle on capital, city
name "Faleion."

8 Corinth. Silver stater ca. 380 B.C.
Obverse: Pegasos drinking from the fountain Peirene.
Reverse: helmeted head of Athena.

9 Barke, Cyrenaica (North Africa). Silver tetrobol ca.
460 B.C.
Obverse: Silphium (a medical plant growing in Cyrenaica). Reverse: head of Zeus Ammon; in the corners,
city name "Bark."

10 Mende, Macedon. Silver tetradrachm, ca. 420 B.C.
Obverse: the god Dionysos, holding his kantharos, re-
cumbent on the back of a donkey. Reverse: city name
"Mendaion" inscribed in the interior of a square, in the
center of which are four palmettes.

11 Mende, Macedon. Bronze coin, ca. 370 B.C.
Obverse: youthful head of the god Dionysos. Reverse:
city name "Men." Amphora between ivy twigs.

12 Katane, Sicily. Silver tetradrachm, ca. 450 B.C.
Obverse: chariot. Reverse: head of Apollo, city name
"Katanai."

13 Himera, Sicily. Silver tetradrachm, ca. 430 B.C.
Obverse: victorious chariot. Reverse: the city goddess sacrificing over flaming altar. To the right, a satyr is bathing in a basin; water is pouring over him from a spout in the shape of a lion's head. Above is a grain of barley.

14 Naxos, Sicily. Silver tetradrachm, ca. 425 B.C.
Obverse: head of the god Dionysos. Reverse: a satyr, holding his thyrsos and drinking wine from a kantharos, is represented squatting on rocky ground out of which grows an ivy plant. To right, city name "Naxion."

15 Syracuse. Silver litra, ca. 470 B.C.
Obverse: head of the nymph Arethusa. Reverse: cuttle-fish, city name "Syra."

Plate III

Classical and Hellenistic Greek Coins

1 Syracuse. Silver decadrachm, ca. 410 B.C.
Obverse: victorious chariot racing to left; above, Nike, the goddess of victory, crowning the charioteer. Below, the prizes for the victor: shield, corslet, greaves, helmet, with the inscription "Athla" (prizes). Reverse: head of the goddess Persephone surrounded by four dolphins; below, the engraver's signature "Euaine."

2 Syracuse. Silver tetradrachm, ca. 410 B.C.
Obverse: a winged goddess in a victorious chariot racing
to right; above, Nike, crowning her; below, the monster
scylla and the signature "Euth." Reverse: head of the
goddess Demeter, surrounded by four dolphins. Above,
city name "Syrako"; below, signature "Eum" (by the
engraver Eumenes).

3 Thurioi, South Italy. Silver nommos, ca. 430 B.C.
Obverse: helmeted head of Athena. Letter "G" (3?).
Reverse: charging bull, fish. Above, city name "Thurion."

4 Tarentum, South Italy. Silver nommos, ca. 370 B.C.
Obverse: naked youth on prancing horse. Reverse: the
youthful founder of the city, Phalanthos, riding a dolphin
and carrying a torch. Below, city name "Taras."

5 Metapontion, South Italy. Small bronze coin, ca. 360 B.C.
Obverse: head of a bald satyr crowned with ivy. Reverse:
ear of barley, city name "Meta."

6 Philip, King of Macedon, 359-336 B.C. Gold stater.
Obverse: head of Apollo. Reverse: chariot drawn by
two horses. Below, the king's name, "Philippou," a trident and a monogram.

7 Lysimachos, King of Thrace, 323-281 B.C. Silver tetradrachm struck at Pergamon (Asia Minor).
Obverse: portrait of Alexander the Great with diadem and the horns of the god Ammon. Reverse: name and title of the king, "Basileos Lysimachou," framing the image of Athena holding a statuette of Nike, who crowns the king's name. In the field, crescent and idol; below, monogram of the moneyer.

8 Demetrios Poliorketes, King of Macedon, 306-283 B.C. Silver tetradrachm struck at Pella.
Obverse: his portrait with bull's horn and diadem. Reverse: "Demetriou Basileos." Poseidon is seated on a rock, holding trident and *aphlaston,* attribute of a naval victory.

9 Antiochos IV Epiphanes, King of Syria (against whom the Maccabees revolted), 175-164 B.C. Silver tetradrachm, struck at Antioch.
Obverse: his portrait. Stars at both ends of his diadem. Reverse: "Basileos Antiochou Theou Epiphanous" ([coin] of the king Antiochos, the resplendent god) framing the image of the enthroned Zeus, holding a statuette of Nike and a scepter.

10 Mithradates VI the Great, the last great adversary of Republican Rome, king of Pontus and Bosporus, 120-63 B.C. Silver tetradrachm.
Obverse: his diademed portrait. Reverse: in a crown of ivy, a drinking Pegasus (cf. Plate II,8) and three-line inscription "Basileos Mithradatou Eupatoros." To left, the emblem of the Pontic kingdom, star and crescent, which later became the Turkish national emblem.

GLOSSARY

Cistophorus	late Hellenistic silver coin of Asia Minor with a "cista mystica" as type
Daric	gold coin showing an archer as type, struck by the Persian kings since Dareios I (522-486 B.C.)
Decadrachm	ten-drachma piece in silver, a large coin struck on special occasions (Athens, Akragas, Syracuse)
Didrachm	two-drachma piece
Diobol	two-obol piece
Drachm	main unit of Greek coinage, divided into six obols
Electrum	alloy of gold and silver, used for coinage mainly in Asia Minor
Hemidrachm	half-drachma piece
Hemiobol	half-obol piece
Litra	Sicilian weight unit (⅕ drachm), later became the Italiote libra (pound)
Mine	unit of weight, = a hundred drachms
Numismatics	the science of coins
Obol	small silver coin of one sixth of a drachm; the name is derived from *obelos* (spit)
Stater	large coin in silver, electrum, or gold, generally weighing two or three drachms
Talent	the largest Greek unit of weight, = 60 mines
Tetradrachm	four-drachm piece, the commonest large Greek silver coin
Tetrobol	four-obol piece
Triobol	three-obol piece

SELECT BIBLIOGRAPHY

B. V. Head, *Historia Numorum* (Oxford: Oxford University Press, 2nd ed., 1911). Still the best handbook on Greek numismatics, but insufficiently illustrated.

C. M. Kraay, *Greek Coins* (London: Thames and Hudson, 1966). An atlas of Max Hirmer's splendid photographs of Greek coins selected mainly for their artistic merit. The text gives good descriptions, the main facts about Greek coinage, and an up-to-date bibliography.

C. T. Seltman, *Greek Coins* (London: Methuen Handbooks, 2nd ed., 1955). A well-illustrated book. The text contains many personal views, sometimes open to discussion and controversy.

7

The Sources

The often heard lament that the sources of antiquities have now run dry is quite unfounded. It is true that many new laws have been passed prohibiting the export of excavation objects from the classical lands of the Mediterranean, but—paradoxically—more antiquities have changed hands and more collections of ancient art have been formed in the last two decades than ever before in history.

Never, in fact, has the commerce in antiquities been as lively as it is today.

Where does this seemingly inexhaustible supply of ancient material come from?

The answer to this question is simple: all antiquities available for purchase come either from old collections or from recent—generally clandestine—excavations.

Let us consider the old collections first. As the great private collections of yesterday are broken up and dispersed, owing to social and economic upheavals, antiquities of every description continue to be thrown onto the market. The Lansdowne marbles, the Hope vases, the Spencer-Churchill bronzes—these

228

are but a few highlights in a long sequence of sales that began in the nineteenth century and continues to the present day. The vast ancient-art holdings of the newspaper magnate William Randolph Hearst were sold at public auction in 1957; other famous private collections to have changed hands recently, such as those of Count Lanckoronski and the late Prince Juritzka, were quietly, and privately, dispersed.

The most important public sales of ancient art take place in London (Sotheby's, Christie's), New York (Sotheby's, Parke-Bernet), Basel (Münzen and Medaillen A.G.), Lucerne (Ars Antiqua A.G.) and Paris (Hotel Drouot), and illustrated catalogs are put out for most of these some weeks in advance. (Those put out by Münzen and Medaillen and by Ars Antiqua are models of their kind.) Lists of prices fetched at past sales are also available on request, and these serve as valuable guidelines to current market values. In addition, the Art Association of America publishes an annual listing of prices realized at most American and European sales.

The collector's luck at antiquities auction sales will, to a great extent, depend on whom he must compete with for bargains; many international art dealers generally attend the more important sales. There are, moreover, certain other disadvantages of the auction over the direct sale: a commission, sometimes as high as 25 percent of the bid, must be added to the purchase price; sales are very often not "free," meaning that bottom limits are set by the owners; and, most important, the auctioneer will generally not assume responsibility for the authenticity of the objects that pass through his hands. (Münzen and Medaillen in Basel is a notable exception.)

It is important not to rely overly on catalog descriptions. The prospective bidder should visit the auction rooms a day or two before the sale if at all possible and personally check each object that he is considering for repairs and restorations. The distinguished name or pedigree of a collection object is not a guarantee that the object is genuine or that it has not at some time been tampered with.

The private sale of antiquities, while gaining rapidly in popularity, is still a somewhat specialized affair. In the United States, art dealers trading exclusively in antiquities exist only in New York and Philadelphia. (See Chapter 10, "Collectors' Guide to the Antiquities Market.") A number of enterprising American art merchants have begun combining ancient art with other collecting areas, such as primitive art and Orientalia. Several galleries on upper Madison Avenue now feature the juxtaposition of ancient and contemporary art; a leading dealer in modern paintings has been staging ancient art exhibits (Cycladic art; Greek vases) for his clients; Brentano's (New York) has taken to mixing the sale of books with antiquities.

In New York the quest for ancient art may take the collector from the fashionable and specialized upper Madison Avenue art dealer to the First Avenue decorator-supplier, with a great many stops along the way. "Finds" are still made in unexpected places. A Greek marble tomb sculpture of exceptional quality was turned up not long ago by a collector at a curio shop on Second Avenue; another collector recently found a rare Roman ivory carving with a downtown carpet dealer.

In Europe there are numbers of small antique dealers in nearly every major city who also handle antiquities. The larger and more specialized antiquities dealers, operating mainly out of Switzerland, comb these sources regularly, so that the chances of discovering an ancient treasure in an out-of-the-way antique shop are rather slim.

Antiquities "hunting," moreover, is a luxury that only the experienced collector should indulge in. Fakes abound (see Chapter 8). About the best advice that can be given to a prospective collector is to buy only from reputable, specialized dealers who know their wares and have established a reputation for standing by every object sold.

A secondary source of bona fide antiquities that might be mentioned is the collector-dealer, or *marchand amateur,* as he is known maliciously by his more professional colleagues. Many collectors maintain their collections in a constant state of flux, selling a piece here, buying another there. Access to these sources is usually by personal introduction.

Finally, mention should be made of antiquities fairs. This recent innovation is becoming increasingly popular in Europe. In London, Paris, Bern, Munich, Florence, and Rome, local and sometimes foreign art dealers assemble annually for a fair, usually lasting one or two weeks, at which they display their finest wares. The Swiss Art and Antiques Fair, held every autumn for ten days at the art museum of Bern, generally includes a good percentage of antiquities. Announcements of antiquities fairs are carried by the leading international art magazines. These fairs are an important index to the market in ancient art—not only as a guide to prices but also because they offer an opportunity to view a good cross section of material currently available.

There is no denying that nearly all fresh finds offered to the collector have left their lands of origin illicitly. It is virtually axiomatic today that wherever there is an official "dig" there is also a flurry of clandestine excavating activity and a flow of archaeological material into the hands of dealers. In Sicily, for example, the Mafia still controls "unofficial" archaeology; in Etruria, the source of most Greek vases that come onto the market nowadays (see Chapter 3), entire communities engage in nocturnal treasure hunts. In Turkey and Greece the situation is much the same; at Burdur in southwest Anatolia, for example, most of the painted terra-cotta revetment of an archaic shrine was removed by dealers during the last five years; around Salonika in Macedonia illegal excavations have been yielding rich finds of ancient jewelry.

The routes taken by clandestinely excavated antiquities to the safe emporiums of Switzerland, Germany, and the United States are as ingenious as they are varied. The art market abounds with tales of exploits involving the transport of antiquities across international frontiers. Some of the methods employed include the concealment of large statuary under bags of cement that are about to be exported. Small bronzes have left Greece concealed in melons—and even through the regular mails. An exquisite gold pendant now in an American collection is reported to have reached its present owner concealed in a lump of Turkish delight.

For many reasons the collector of antiquities will be well advised never to buy fresh finds in the lands where they are found, and above all never to engage in their removal abroad. First, there is the danger of being caught. We must not forget that whereas the purchase of antiquities is legal in many Mediterranean countries, their export generally is *not*. Second, whereas it is true that "the man on the spot" will often sell to a private collector at prices only slightly above those he charges to the trade, he will also often maintain a stock of forgeries to be disposed of profitably to the unwitting amateur. The antiquity "picked up for a song" from the local innkeeper near an excavation site will more often than not turn out to be a fake. The same unfortunately also holds true for many of the "bargains" made in the bazaars of Athens, Istanbul, and Izmir, or at many of the innumerable small dealers to be found in Rome.

The fragmenting and dispersal of archaeological finds obviously poses a moral as well as a legal problem. There is no denying that much important scientific information is lost forever when a tomb is pillaged. Clandestine digging has tended of late to develop a conscience of a sort in its own interest, however, and outright vandalism is becoming increasingly rare. Whereas formerly treasure hunters sought only precious metal, today even the smallest scrap of pottery found in a tomb is carefully preserved: nowadays, even fragments are at a premium.

One might go so far as to say that the trade in art objects has in numerous cases actually preserved works of art that would otherwise have been destroyed. In many parts of Turkey, for example, ancient marbles are still cherished as building material, and it is often only their cash value that keeps them out of the lime kilns. In South Italy an important lead inscription of the Archaic period was about to be melted into buckshot by its discoverers when an art dealer happened on the scene and purchased it. In Greece as well as Italy, a farmer who discovers an antiquity on his land will more often than not destroy it forthwith (if he cannot sell it) in order to avoid the suspicion of engaging in illegal excavation.

The lack of enlightened antiquities policies on the part of the governments concerned is responsible in large measure for the anarchical situation that still exists in many areas of the Mediterranean. Fortunately, however, official authorities are beginning to wake up to their responsibilities. In Italy groping steps are being taken to legalize the supervised export of certain types of antiquities while at the same time tightening up control over unauthorized excavation. The Italian government only recently opened an official outlet in Rome for the sale of genuine antiquities that have been examined by a committee of experts and found to be dispensable. The process for indemnifying farmers for turning in chance finds is being streamlined; at the same time joint patrols of archaeological inspectors and police periodically visit all known dealers and antiquities shops in order to make sure that registers are being kept and sales of registered antiquities reported. Similar measures are being introduced in Greece and Turkey with encouraging results.

8

How to Detect a Forgery

It would be foolish to pretend that the detection of forgeries can be learned from reading a manual on the subject. I do not know a collector—or even a museum curator, for that matter—who has not, at some time or another, been taken in by a forgery. It is only by restricting purchases to a narrow and well-documented field that one can be relatively safe from error. But what an uninspiring prospect! To "play it safe" and never to take a chance is tantamount to resigning oneself to collecting mediocrities.

Perhaps more than in any other area of collecting, the market in ancient art is riddled with fakes. They range from ingenious and technically well-made products to the ludicrous plaster casts peddled as originals on flea markets the world over. It is against this background of lurking danger that the collector must learn to sharpen his eye and his wits.

WHAT IS A FORGERY?

In ninety-nine cases out of a hundred, forgeries are created with the deliberate intent to deceive and defraud. It can happen, however, that an honest artist or artisan is duped into producing an imitation that is later sold as an antiquity without his knowledge. One such case with which I am personally familiar involved a Levantine goldsmith who was commissioned to produce a sporting trophy. The "trophy" appeared on the art market shortly after it was completed and was sold as a unique antiquity complete with pedigree and scholarly documentation.

Fortunately, most forgeries are fairly easy to detect, for the present-day forger is interested in quantity rather than quality. With the vast numbers of tourists traveling the world today and looking for antiquities bargains, he knows that his greatest profit lies in numbers. Over 90 percent of all forgeries currently produced come out of a few specialized ateliers located in Greece, Italy, Syria, and Lebanon.

THE "PASTICCIO" AND THE RESTORED WORK OF ART

Far more insidious than the outright forgery are the restored work of art and the *pasticcio. Pasticcio* is the Italian word for hodgepodge. In the language of art and archaeology, it refers to a work composed of various alien elements combined so as to create the semblance of an intact object. Often fragments of various poorly preserved but genuine objects will be combined so as to create a salable piece. Such "improvements" may range from the restoration of missing parts to the addition of alien accessories, inscriptions, and even painted or carved details. Thus, for example, a Corinthian aryballos with a simple linear decoration (such as can be bought at most antiquities dealers for under a hundred dollars) will receive an additional decoration—a roaring lion or a cockfight—so as to become some unwary collector's "find." Reputable dealers generally instruct their restorers to render all modern additions or restorations clearly recognizable for what they are. Unfortunately, not all dealers are reputable, and not all restorers honest.

THE PEDIGREE AND THE EXPERTISE

A well-known collector, when questioned about his remarkable success in avoiding the purchase of forgeries, replied, "I never buy a story." This would seem to be an axiom for *any* collector to follow. It applies to the pedigree as well as to the professional expertise. The most reliable sources can deceive; the most scholarly expertise can be mistaken. That an antiquity once graced the mantle-piece of a Count Sabouroff or a Prince Napoleon does not in itself prove that it is genuine. The most venerable of aristocratic collections contain their share of fakes. Rarely, moreover, is an important fake sold without at least one expert opinion.

Just as one should never "buy a story," one must never allow one's judgment to be influenced by an elegant setting designed to inspire confidence. Resist flattering lighting; insist on examining the piece you are considering for purchase by the light of day; do not allow your opinion of a work of art to be swayed by the personality of the vendor.

THE TECHNICAL EXAMINATION

Nearly every major forgery sold in recent years has been accompanied not only by scholarly expertise but also by a laboratory report presenting conclusive evidence of the object's authenticity.

A genuine work of art speaks for itself. As often as not, a piece offered with elaborate expertise or a laboratory report has at some time been doubted by a competent authority—and generally with good reason.

We must be clear in our minds about the limitations of technical criteria in judging the authenticity of a work of art. A laboratory examination or analysis can establish the composition of a metal, the crystalline structure of a stone, the alignment of particles in a terra-cotta. It *cannot,* by itself, tell us what we really want to know: Is the piece genuine? To answer this crucial question, the element of subjective human judgment is indispensable. Technical data must be interpreted by an expert intimately familiar with the technique of ancient art—and of its modern imitations. There are in the entire world but a handful of technicians qualified to pass this kind of judgment, and even they are not infallible. It is by no means unusual, therefore, that obvious and outrageous fakes will pass sophisticated laboratory tests with flying colors while, conversely, perfectly genuine objects will continue to be condemned.

CONDITIONED INTUITION

While book learning can supply valuable insights into the meaning of a work of art, its place in history, its style, it cannot afford complete protection against the clever imitation. Often museum curators will take an object, submitted to them for an opinion, in their hands, turn it over once or twice, and pronounce judgment ("genuine" or "fake"). When asked to explain, they are apt to be at a loss for words, and if pressed further will frequently admit that it is no more than a feeling. This *feeling,* precisely when it is conditioned by experience, is of inestimable value in determining the authenticity of a work of art.

STONE SCULPTURE

The foolproof test for the authenticity of ancient stone sculpture has yet to be invented. To date, no existing machine or device can eliminate the judgment of experts in lapidary questions: connoisseurship still holds the field.

Much valuable technical evidence can, of course, be gleaned about the physical properties of the work in question, and such information should be intelligently evaluated and applied.

For example, the presence or absence of "rootmarks," usually on the under-cut areas—ears, hair, drapery folds—of a piece of purportedly ancient sculpture remains a valuable criterion. Rootmarks, thought to be petrified root fibers, have the appearance of delicate fibrous tracery covering the surface of the stone, and are generally harder than the stone to which they have attached themselves. Forgers have yet to duplicate this curious natural phenomenon successfully. The most convincing modern "rootmarks" ever encountered by this writer could easily be removed with the tip of a pocketknife: they proved to made of wax.

One should always be wary of a sculpture that shows no visible signs of age. Never accept on faith the claim that a work has been "overcleaned" by its last owner. Be wary also of sandy "deposits," as well as of deposits that give the appearance of having been concocted with plaster of Paris or glue. Watch also for splotchy purplish discolorations of the surface of the marble. These are the telltale traces of "aging" with potassium permanganate, the hallmark of some of the most recent forgeries to come from Italy.

The stone of which a piece is carved is another important index to its authenticity. A Greek sculpture of the fifth century, for example, can never be carved of Italian Carrara marble because the quarries at Carrara were not worked until Roman times. It therefore pays to familiarize oneself with the materials employed by sculptors in antiquity. Beware of "Magna Graecia"—Greek South Italy and Sicily—as a stylistic alibi for a work that aspires to being Greek but lacks the necessary stylistic qualifications. This region, which, owing to a dearth of good quarries, produced little marble sculpture in ancient times, has become a favorite catchall to explain the stylistic anomalies of modern forgeries.

The portable ultraviolet lamp, available from most suppliers of surgical equipment, is an invaluable aid in determining whether a sculpture has been restored, recut, or otherwise tampered with. The application of ultraviolet rays in the examination of works of art has been discussed by the late J. J. Rorimer in a fundamental monograph on the subject. *(Ultraviolet Rays and Their Use in the Examination of Works of Art.* Metropolitan Museum, New York, 1931.)

Cycladic Idols

A very common variety of marble forgery likely to be encountered today is the imitation Cycladic idol. The current proliferation of Cycladic fakes is readily explainable on two counts: (1) the originals are in great vogue and fetch high prices; and (2) being simple abstract forms, virtually devoid of modeling, these works are far easier to imitate than, say, the portrait of a Roman lady with an elaborate coiffure.

A New York dealer confided a "foolproof" test for Cycladic idols to me, and I shall pass it along for what it is worth. Hold the object between thumb and forefinger and strike it lightly on a doorsill, like a tuning fork. A forgery will emit a clear bell-like ring, whereas a genuine idol emits a dull thump. It is, of course, necessary to experiment with both genuine and imitation idols in order to accustom one's ear to the proper sound. (I must admit that I have not yet mastered the technique.) More reliable tests for the authenticity of Cycladic idols have recently been developed by the laboratory of the Prähistorische Staatssammlung, Munich.

BRONZES

There are more forgeries made in bronze than in any other material, and it is in this area of ancient art that inexperienced collectors fall down most frequently and suffer their keenest disappointments. These forgeries usually take the form of small statuettes. Utilitarian bronzes, such as vessels and their attachments, tools, and weapons, are less commonly imitated, although enough forgeries of such works exist as well.

The criteria for judging the authenticity of statuettes and other works in bronze are threefold: style, technique, and surface. Style falls outside the framework of this discussion (a number of good handbooks on the subject exist). I might, however, repeat my earlier exhortation: Go to the museum; look and compare! As for the technique, a basic familiarity with the ancient casting processes (cf. p. 80) is essential, for this is where nine out of ten forgeries fall down.

Briefly: The multiple-cast mold in general use today was not employed for casting statuette bronzes in classical antiquity. Greek, Roman, and Etruscan bronze statuettes, whether cast solid or hollow, are invariably unique creations. Never are there any two alike. The clay mold from which they were made was broken up in the process of removing the finished bronze; consequently there are no casting seams. This is not the case with most bronze forgeries, which are produced by the modern technique from plaster section molds, which can be reused many times. Casting seams, or their traces, can usually be detected somewhere on virtually any modern cast bronze forgery. In the more careful forgeries, the seams are generally effaced by filing. Look, therefore, for telltale filemarks, especially on the arms and legs of a figurine. A good hand lens is, of course, essential.

Perhaps the commonest single class of objects brought to curators of ancient art for appraisal are the excellent reproductions of bronzes in the Naples National Museum, formerly made—as tourist souvenirs and free of all intent to deceive—by the firm of G. Sommer and Sons. An illustrated catalog of their wares exists and is most instructive. The standard museum reproduction has a typical, somewhat bilious chemical patina, but frequently these objects are repatinated and provided with suitably convincing "incrustation."

Such items are really not worthy of being called forgeries; they remain reproductions, even when they are sold with fraudulent intent. The detection of more sophisticated bronze forgeries can be very difficult. Statuettes are generally modeled on authentic works in various materials, including marbles. Sometimes various parts or aspects of several originals will be combined. In such cases, the forger, usually lacking a full understanding of his subject in all its stylistic and iconographic complexities, is apt to fall down on details. He may, for example, combine the hairstyle of a certain stylistic phase with a rendering of anatomy that is too primitive or too advanced for the period.

Even the cleverest forger will often fail when called upon to display artistic talent. Look carefully at engraving and other fine surface details, for these generally are the giveaways. If the modeling of a figure is exquisite but the engraved details (which cannot be copied by any mechanical process) are crude, beware!

Patina

The color of unpatinated bronze ranges from yellow to orange—the color of sun-bronzed skin. It is generally believed that Greek bronzes were polished and kept free of oxidation in antiquity in much the same way that we polish brass and silver today. Natural patination of a bronze is the result of gradual changes in the chemistry of the "skin," or surface, of the metal under the influence of the environment to which it is exposed. The relative presence or absence of certain minerals in the soil in which a bronze has lain for centuries can produce profound variations in the color and texture of its surface. Thus, for example, a bronze found in the soil of Olympia will have a characteristic mottled blue-gray "Olympia" patina, whereas a second bronze, made in the same atelier as the first but found in Corinth, may be uniformly olive green.

It used to be true that with some practice one could always recognize a forgery by its evenly colored chemical patina, which could be easily scraped off with a pocketknife, leaving a whitish powder; and many chemical patinas will indeed produce a telltale stain when rubbed with a piece of cotton soaked in one of several solvents. (Alcohol, benzine, and acetone are recommended, in that order.) This is no longer true, however, except for the lowest order of "tourist" forgeries. Forgers presently working in Rome, Beirut, Athens, and elsewhere, have succeeded in artificially patinating bronzes with a degree of refinement that makes this form of simple detection an impossibility.

Methods for imitating ancient patinas range from exposure to corrosive fumes, such as those of ammonia, to immersion in diluted acid. Even more sophisticated methods of patinating bronze forgeries include burying the product under a dung heap. An Italian "specialist" in the field has perfected a technique whereby the surface of the bronze is irritated so as to produce within a few days a patina that does not differ visibly from one produced by the action of centuries.

A dealer taught me a simple method for testing the authenticity of an ancient bronze. It was taught him, he said, by his father, a noted antiquary in his day. Since I find that this amazingly simple and effective test is not widely known, I repeat it for what it is worth:

To a 20 percent solution of hydrochloric acid add filings of patina taken from an ancient bronze (corroded coins do very well for this purpose) until the acid has been completely neutralized. Strain the pungent green liquid thus obtained, and dilute with an equal amount of water. Now lay bare a small, inconspicuous area of the bronze to be tested, using a sharp scalpel. Apply a drop of the testing liquid to the exposed surface of the bronze, and allow it to evaporate. An ancient bronze will form a new patina under the influence of this chemical provocation within twenty-four hours. A modern bronze will merely dull.

I have tried it and it works. It is, incidentally, essential to remove any wax or lacquer from the surface of the bronze prior to applying the testing solution.

VASES

Fake Greek vases are perhaps the most easily identified class of antiquities forgeries the collector is liable to encounter. Whereas authentic Greek vases are decorated in the so-called "black-glaze" technique, a complicated and exacting firing process (see p. 109), most imitations, particularly the older ones, are painted with oil-base pigments and/or lacquers. Whereas true "black-glaze" is virtually indestructible (it can be subjected to strong acids without damage), imitation glazes generally disintegrate in solvents such as acetone, alcohol, or benzine. A good test is to rub an inconspicuous area of a suspected forgery with a piece of white cotton dipped in solvent; if black adheres to the cloth, the vase should be subjected to closer examination.

A more drastic manner of determining the truth is to immerse the vase overnight in softened water. (Any commercial water softener, such as Calgon, can be used; the powder is added to the water bath until the water becomes "slippery" between the fingers). If the "glaze" dissolves, it was modern. This treatment, it should be pointed out, has the disadvantage of also dissolving any honest restorations, and possibly ancient matte-painted decoration, in the process.

A less drastic technique is the "fire test." The area to be examined is rubbed with lighter fluid, ignited, and held for a few seconds over a low flame. If the "glaze" is oil paint or lacquer, as suspected, it will now readily yield to light rubbing with a cloth dipped in solvent. If the glaze is ancient, the surface will remain unaffected. The technique requires some practice, and great care must be taken not to ignite one's hair or clothing.

The detection of spurious Greek vases will doubtless become increasingly difficult. Attic black-glaze, long considered inimitable, has now been successfully duplicated, and the first specimens of technically perfect "Attic glaze" forgeries are at the time of writing beginning to appear on the market. Fortunately for the collector, the quality of their drawing still leaves much to be desired.

TERRA-COTTAS

Clay is the cheapest and most readily available of all artistic raw materials, and the technique of working it has changed little over the ages. It is only to be expected, therefore, that the problem of distinguishing between old and new in this medium will be even more hazardous than when dealing with stone or bronze.

The difficulties are compounded by the fact that ancient molds for the production of terra-cotta figures and reliefs have survived in considerable numbers and have in some instances fallen into the hands of forgers.

Terra-cotta forgeries intended for today's sophisticated market are frequently fired in primitive kilns virtually identical with those used in antiquity. Even the earth colors applied to terra-cottas by talented forgers are practically indistinguishable from those of originals. Nor is the presence or absence of surface deposit, or "incrustation," a sure index to authenticity: ancient terra-cottas were often deposited in well-constructed tombs, and therefore need not necessarily have been exposed to patinating or incrusting elements (ground water, salts, and so forth). When "incrustation" is present, it is generally a gray, fine-grained, and tenaciously hard silicious deposit. Beware of "sandy" deposits that can be easily brushed off; they are more often than not sand mixed with glue.

I know of only one reliable "home" test for the authenticity of an ancient terra-cotta: its *smell.* When dipped in water, an ancient terra-cotta, regardless of its provenience or whether or not it has actually lain buried in the soil, will emit an agreeably earthy fragrance not unlike that of a freshly ploughed field. It is the fragrance of antiquity. A modern terra-cotta is generally nearly odorless.

Fired clay can now be dated by thermoluminescence, but the number of institutions equipped for this sophisticated test are few.

Perhaps the most common group of terra-cotta forgeries are those of "Tanagra" figurines (see pp. 167 - 169), produced toward the end of the last century. These imitations can today be readily detected, and they have, by and large, been removed from museum exhibitions. Yet a surprisingly large number are still sold each year to private collectors. Forged "Tanagras" are more thin-walled, and hence lighter in the hand, than the originals. They emit a hollow ring when tapped with the finger. Their clay differs from the clay of genuine figurines by virtue of the relatively coarse grain and brick-red (rather than ocher) color. The applied color also differs, particularly the black: held in a raking light, the black of a genuine Tanagra assumes a brownish hue; that of the imitation reflects jet- or blue-black.

Even more treacherous than these outright forgeries are the *pasticcios*—terra-cottas assembled from various alien parts. Look at the necks of figurines with particularly close attention. Is there a telltale smear? If so, the "intact" example may turn out to have an alien, or possibly modern, head. The same is true of limbs, drapery folds, and so on. Here the ultraviolet lamp is an invaluable aid: used properly, it can reveal clearly if and where an ancient terracotta has been tampered with in modern times (see p. 237).

GOLD JEWELRY

A museum curator recently confided to me, "I wouldn't touch anything made of gold." This fear of gold is shared by many collectors, and it is justified: an appalling number of fakes in precious metal have entered museum and private collections in recent years.

The tendency is to view jewelry as adornment rather than art. The sheer voluptuous luxury of gold can blind the judgment of the keenest eye. When approached with the same critical scrutiny that we reserve for other media, gold jewelry will be found to be neither more nor less "dangerous" than any other works of art.

Some knowledge of ancient goldsmithing technique is indispensable for anyone seriously considering collecting in this problematic field.

A few observations may serve to give the prospective collector of Greek jewelry a notion of the importance of technological data in determining authenticity. Ancient gold wire, for example, is always handmade; that is to say, it is generally either *strip-twisted* (produced from a flat strip of sheet gold by twisting until it is round in much the way that a paper drinking straw is made) or *forged* from a strip by rolling and hammering. The little irregularities that characterize such handmade wire contribute much to the beauty of Greek jewelry. The wires of modern jewelry forgeries, on the other hand, are generally mechanically produced with the aid of a *drawplate*, an instrument not known until the high Middle Ages. A strip-twisted wire—and by far most wires employed in Greek jewelry are of this variety—will exhibit under magnification characteristic spiral striations on its surface—the vestiges of the manufacturing process. A wire produced with a drawplate is cold and mechanical by comparison. The difference is easily recognizable when an ancient piece and a modern imitation are examined side by side under a strong magnifying lens.

The diameter of filigree wires is another important index to the authenticity of Greek goldwork. Greek filigree, particularly that used during the Hellenistic period, is generally very fine; modern filigree will be found under magnification to be coarser.

The same applies to *granulation.* Modern granulation can in most instances be distinguished from the ancient product with the aid of a good hand lens. The individual beads of ancient granulation generally consist of perfect spheres invisibly "welded" to their background. (For the technique, recently rediscovered, see pp. 180-181). The granulation of modern gold forgeries is generally attached with some form of solder (that is, an alloy having a lower melting point), and the granules themselves appear to "sag."

In the past, forgers in precious metal tended to work on the grand scale. The tendency today is to produce great numbers of small and relatively insignificant pieces that will not attract attention. A workshop situated in Syria or Lebanon has of late been producing quantities of "Hellenistic" and "Roman" earrings. The gold content of these pieces is minimal, and they are often sold for less than the price of moderately expensive costume jewelry.

Finally, as in all other fields of ancient art, the importance of studying originals cannot be overemphasized. The museums of Athens, Berlin, Munich, London, Paris, and New York have representative collections of Greek jewelry displayed in a manner such as to permit close study. Few serious forgers of Greek jewelry nowadays "invent." Their works tend to be copies or variations of well-documented jewelry types represented in museum collections. Very elaborate or unusual pieces should accordingly arouse suspicion. Jewelry *sets,* in particular, should be treated with utmost caution.

In conclusion, the best defense against the purchase of fakes is to study them. Handle and examine recognized forgeries wherever possible (at dealers' rooms, in museum offices, and in the homes of friends). Nearly all museums keep photographic files on forgeries that have been offered for purchase and rejected, and most are only too happy to share this invaluable information with serious collectors. Most forgeries produced today conform to certain patterns, and these will become apparent once the eye is adjusted.

Buying from well-known and reputable dealers, who can be held accountable for their merchandise (see Chapter 7, "The Sources"), constitues the best protection against the purchase of forgeries. Unless you are an expert, never buy an expensive antiquity from an unknown source without consulting a museum with a curatorial staff member specialized in ancient art. In the United States, these museums are to be found in Baltimore, Boston, Brooklyn, Cambridge (Fogg Museum of Art), Cleveland, New York, and Philadelphia.

9

The Care and Conservation of Antiquities

Many a work of art has been ruined by improper care. The following hints may be helpful to the collector.

MARBLE

Ordinary dirt can be removed from an ancient marble by washing with a commercial solvent. Proper rinsing is again of utmost importance, since otherwise the surface may be dulled. Distilled water should be used for the final soaking, preferably for at least a day and a night. Great care must be taken when washing coarse crystalline marble, such as that from the island of Paros, lest the surface crumble. The removal of hard incrustations and "rootmarks" from an ancient marble should be entrusted to an expert. The use of acids is to be discouraged, for there is danger of "skinning" the stone. The best method is still the old-fashioned one: careful chipping and picking with special tools. For a large piece of sculpture an infinite amount of patience is required.

BRONZES

Like vases and terra-cottas, ancient bronzes are often covered with unsightly granular incrustation when found. The beautiful green or bluish patina that we have come to associate with ancient bronzes lies underneath this outer protective layer.

It should be said at the outset that, while superficial deposit can be removed without hurting the patina by soaking in Calgon and washing thoroughly in distilled water, there is no quick and easy way to clean a corroded bronze, no substitute for long experience. A skilled restorer may take weeks or even months to clean a single statuette. Restorers today generally employ a combination of several techniques, varying from case to case. Of those I have talked to, most agree that the best basic method is still that employed for the last hundred years, namely, working "cold," or carefully scraping the surface with a special tool. This is a demanding and time-consuming task that should never be attempted by an inexperienced hand. The specialist knows exactly how close the metal can be "shaved"; he knows that the difference between a beautiful and lustrous patina and a mutilated or dead surface may lie in a crucial hundredth of a millimeter.

The use of *acids* for cleaning ancient bronzes is to be shunned. Nor can the immersion in an *ultrasonic vibration tank* (such as now exist in several portable models) be endorsed without reservation. A collector friend recently ruined a fine bronze the day after he acquired it by subjecting it to this drastic method of cleaning. *Electrolysis* can be recommended only as a last resort, for the conservation of bronzes exhibiting deep pitting and active "bronze disease." Such treatment, again, is best left to a specialist.

Humidity is the mortal enemy of ancient bronzes. Under humid conditions, especially during the summer months, a healthy bronze may suddenly break out in bright green spots that spread rapidly if not checked. In a bronze afflicted with *bronze disease* the cuprous chloride which gives the patina its beautiful green color becomes transformed into whitish cupric chloride. The metal becomes soft and mushy and sheds a fine whitish powder which, incidentally, is deadly poison if swallowed, inhaled, or allowed to penetrate the skin.

The best prevention against bronze disease is a dry environment and constant temperature. Several brands of silicate gel desiccating crystals are available from chemical supply houses. These blue crystals, which turn pink when saturated, should be placed in an open or perforated container in the case containing ancient bronzes. The crystals should be changed as soon as their color has changed. They can be reused indefinitely by drying in an ordinary oven (the color changes back to blue).

An afflicted bronze must be isolated from other bronzes immediately and treated without delay. Treatment usually involves both chemical and mechanical processes, and is best entrusted to a trained technician benefiting from the facilities of a specialized research laboratory. Only in extreme cases is the electrolytical or chemical "stripping" of an ancient bronze justified.

Here are a few tips concerning the handling and conservation of ancient bronzes:

There are two conflicting theories concerning handling. Some experts feel that excessive handling is ruinous to the surface of a bronze; one purist, a well-known collector, even goes so far as to don white gloves before opening a case. Others feel that frequent handling actually enhances the beauty of a patina. I tend to side with the purist, for there can be no question but that a beautiful light patina can be stained or darkened by sweaty fingers. Be sure that your hands are dry when handling *any* work of ancient art; otherwise pick the object up with a handkerchief. This applies especially to bronzes and terra-cottas.

Some collectors (and museums) spray their bronzes with varnish or other surface isolators (Cryptolac and Acrylac are two of the best-known products manufactured specifically for this purpose). While this treatment does form a barrier to the action of air and dampness, it may actually have detrimental effects in the long run, namely, by forcing incipient bronze disease "underground" rather than allowing it to come to the surface where it can be seen and treated. Synthetic isolators also give ancient bronzes an unpleasant lacquered appearance.

POTTERY

Pottery is fragile, especially if it has been previously mended. Greek vases particularly should never be picked up by the handle or by the rim (particularly cups). Always cradle the vase with both hands, and never handle more than one at a time. When setting a vase down, lower it gently so as to avoid chipping; if placing it in a glass vitrine, watch out for the shelf above.

When a Greek vase is freshly found, it is usually covered with a stubborn layer of calcium incrustation and often by a network of tough "rootmarks" as well. The incrustation is due to the presence of calcium in the soil. If a vase is acquired in a "virgin" state—that is to say, if it has not been cleaned already by the dealer through whose hands it has passed—the removal of this unsight- ly incrustation, which is apt to obscure the decoration, presents no problem if attacked in the right way. If the incrustation is of the flaky variety, it will gen- erally yield to soaking for a day or two in water softened with a commercial water softener such as Calgon (detergents are not to be recommended). It is important to rinse the piece well after this treatment, preferably for at least twenty-four hours in a bucket placed under a running tap and padded with sponges or rags, to prevent surface bruising.

This method failing, dilute hydrochloric acid, obtainable at any drugstore, can be safely applied to any Greek vase with a glazed surface. (The cleaning of white-ground lekythoi [cf. pp. 128-129] should never be attempted by an amateur.) The incrustation will generally disappear within a few hours; if it does not yield, a stronger concentration, applied locally by repeated pouring from a beaker, can be tried. When cleaning a vase of porous clay with acid, proper water- ing is vitally important: every trace of acid must leave the clay, since otherwise a deterioration of the clay surface—sometimes noticeable only after a lapse of years—may result. Rinse for twenty-four hours or more, as above.

The "do-it-yourself" assembly and restoration of a vase acquired in frag- ments can be quite time-consuming, and presupposes a certain degree of manual skill. The fragments, or sherds, must be thoroughly cleaned, especially the joining surfaces. Often, vases have been restored badly by a previous owner. Sherds may be wrongly joined, inserted in the wrong places, or even borrowed from other pots. In such cases it may be necessary to take the vase apart entirely and to begin the restoration afresh. This is best done by placing it overnight in softened water, resting it on cushions, in the case of a larger vase, to prevent fragments from bruising. Remains of old adhesive may be removed with benzine, acetone, or alcohol (for shellac), depending on the nature of the adhesive em- ployed. A decorated vase can be assembled in the manner of a jigsaw puzzle, filling in the design piece by piece. Where there is little decoration, some practice and a knowledge of shapes are required. Wheelmarks on the inside surface of the sherd are a valuable guide. The thickness of the clay is also important in helping to decide where two sherds belong in a given pot.

Any celluloid-base cement, such as Duco, can be employed for joining. I prefer to use two concentrations: a thin one (mixed with twenty parts acetone) and a thick one (about one to five). Several brushings of the joining surfaces with the thin solution, allowing the cement to soak in and dry between applications, will ensure a strong bond. For the final joint, a fine line of the concentrated cement is applied to one break only, and the two fragments are firmly squeezed together until the cement has set—a matter of about a minute.

Some ceramic restorers use a sandbox for assembling a vase from sherds. The sandbox is, in fact, indispensable for the assembly of open shapes, such as cups and bowls. Globular shapes, especially the larger vases, such as hydrias, can sometimes be most easily assembled with the aid of rubber bands. In this manner, imperfectly matched joints may be corrected by softening with acetone and gentle squeezing.

Filling gaps with plaster has become easier since the introduction, some years ago, of water-soluble plasters and specking cements. Where the gaps are large, a plastoline mold can be made from a preserved area of equal form and curvature. The approved practice today is to tint the plaster a shade darker or lighter than the clay of the vase itself, so that the restoration will be easily recognizable as such without being obtrusive.

TERRA-COTTAS

The proper method for removing dirt or incrustation from a fired but unpainted terra-cotta is essentially the same as that described above for pottery. The terra-cotta must be well cushioned with sponges or rags while soaking, for even a well-baked statuette is apt to become soft and friable when waterlogged. Extreme care must be taken when lifting a wet terra-cotta.

Stubborn incrustation can generally be dissolved with acid. Never, however, apply acid to a dry terra-cotta; acid poured over a waterlogged terra-cotta will affect only the exterior, without penetrating deeply into the clay. Be sure to rinse well! Terra-cottas that have been inadequately watered after cleaning have an unpleasant habit of "blossoming" out in fine white saline crystals, sometimes several years later.

It is better to underclean terra-cottas than to overclean them. A thin film of incrustation can actually be desirable, like a fine patina on a bronze, in that it helps accentuate the contours. A layer of white on a terra-cotta is often the original engobe layer, and should not be removed.

The powdery surface of a poorly baked terra-cotta can be "fixed" with beeswax emulsion or caseine. Caseine has the advantage of being invisible if properly applied. Several applications of thin caseine emulsion will consolidate, and thus salvage, even a crumbling statuette.

RESTORERS

In the New York area Joseph Ternbach in Great Neck, Long Island, enjoys an international reputation as a restorer of ancient bronzes. Marcel Gibrat at 1266B Madison Avenue, Manhattan (FI 8-0319), formerly of the Metropolitan Museum's conservation staff, is at the time of writing the only American private restorer specializing in Greek pottery. William Young, head of the Boston Museum of Fine Arts' Research Laboratory, accepts objects from private collectors. His department is also specialized in the examination of works of ancient art. In Europe the firm of Lekythos A.G. at Malzgasse 12, Basel, Switzerland, is equipped to deal with ancient bronzes, terra-cottas, and vases. The Maison Andrée in Paris specializes in the restoration of bronzes. Restorers equipped for dealing with large marble sculptures are employed by the museums of Munich and Copenhagen; both institutions accept private commissions as their work schedule permits.

SELECT BIBLIOGRAPHY

J. Charbonneaux, *Greek Bronzes* (New York: The Studio Publications, 1962), 143 ff. Contains expert conservation advice, as well as valuable hints on the display of ancient bronzes.

R. M. Cook, *Greek Painted Pottery* (London: Methuen, 1960), 280ff., has a chapter of practical comments for the vase collector.

H. J. Plenderleith, *The Conservation of Antiquities and Works of Art* (New York: Oxford University Press, 1956). By the retired head of the British Museum's restoration department. Still the most useful general work on the subject, a "must" for anyone wishing to resort to self-help.

10

Collectors' Guide to the Antiquities Market

This list is selective; it comprises only accredited dealers actually specializing in ancient art and implies no guarantee whatsoever for the authenticity of works of art purchased. A comprehensive listing of antiquities and antique dealers in America and abroad is contained in *International Antiques Yearbook* (1968-1969), edited by Philip Wilson.

UNITED STATES OF AMERICA

New York

J. J. Klejman Gallery (Mr. and Mrs. J. J. Klejman), 982 Madison Avenue, Tel. LE 5-5484. The Klejmans maintain a large and varied stock of antiquities in every price range, and have sold important works of ancient art to the leading museums and private collectors of America.

Komor Gallery (Mathias Komor), 19 East Seventy-first Street, Tel. TR 9-3840. By appointment only. Mr. Komor is well known in American collecting circles for his excellent taste and absolute reliability. His objects tend to range in price between $500 and $5,000.

Royal-Athena Galleries (Jerome M. Eisenberg), 1066 Madison Avenue, Tel. 861-4133. Antiquities at cut rate: a treasure trove for the collector with only $50 to spend.

Philadelphia

Hesperia Art (George Allen), 2219 St. James Place, Tel. (215) LO 7-6533. By appointment only. Reliable source of low- and middle-priced antiquities, including coins, pottery, glass, bronzes, terra-cottas, engraved gems, and occasionally even sculptures in marble. Publishes monthly illustrated stock list *(Hesperia Art Bulletin),* available by subscription for $2.00 annually.

GREAT BRITAIN

London

Spink and Son, Ltd., 5-7 King St., W.1, Tel. WHI-5275. Mr. S. R. Mathews is now in charge of the ancient-art department of this old and respected firm. The quality of the material varies greatly; occasionally a good find can be made here, especially in classical sculpture.

FRANCE

Paris

Galerie Archéologie (Dr. Elie Borowski), 40, rue du Bac, 7e, Tel. LIT-6160. The Paris subsidiary of the well-known Basel dealer; objects of certified authenticity in the middle to lower price range.

Galerie Segredakis (N. Koutoulakis), 4 rue de l'Echelle, 1e, Tel. OPE-6563.

Orient-Occident (M. Dupras, 5, rue des Sts.-Pères, 6e, Tel. LIT-6648. The owner is a qualified Egyptologist, and his gallery accordingly specializes in Egyptian art. Occasionally attractive Greek and Roman objects also turn up here.

GERMANY

Frankfort-am-Main

Dr. Kurt Deppert, Mauerweg 12, Tel. 491769. By appointment only. Reliable source of Greek and Roman coins, vases, and minor arts. Dr. Deppert is a professional archaeologist. Illustrated lists, with prices, available on application.

Galerie für griechische und römische Kunst (M. Yeganeh), Taunusstrasse 52 (near railway station), Tel. 251778.

Köln (Cologne)

Dr. Horst-Ulbo Bauer, Neuenhofer Allee, 10, Tel. 417559. By appointment only. Greek, Etruscan, Roman, and Near Eastern art.

Munich

Antiken H. Herzer & Co. (Dr. H. Herzer), St.-Annastrasse 12, Tel. 297730.

HOLLAND

Amsterdam

Jacques Schulman, Numismaat (Mrs. Jacques Schulman), Keizersgracht 448, Tel. 233380. Mrs. Schulman continues her late husband's prestigious numismatic firm and has recently branched out into the Greek, Roman, and Etruscan minor arts. Greek and Etruscan terra-cottas are a specialty. Coin lists available on application.

ITALY

Rome

Barsanti, Antichità (M. Barsanti), Via Margutta, 46. Specializes in ancient sculpture and decorative art.

Fallani (Giorgio Fallani), Via del Babuino 58a, Tel. 689700. One of Rome's most serious antiquities dealers, with a varied stock of objects (vases, terra-cottas, bronzes, marbles, glyptic arts).

Simotti-Rocchi, Antichità (Marcello Simotti-Rocchi), Largo Fontanelle Borghese (across from the Borghese palace), Tel. 565109.

SWITZERLAND

Ascona

Galleria Casa Serodine (Dr. W. Rosenbaum), Tel. 21861. The seventeenth-century palace that houses the gallery alone is worth a visit to Ascona. Bargains may still occasionally be found here, especially in Greek, Etruscan, and South Italian ceramics, bronzes, and terra-cottas.

Basel

Dr. Elie Borowski, Angensteinerstrasse 7, Tel. 410834. By appointment only. Select objects of classical art and archaeology.

Münzen und Medaillen A.G. (Dr. Herbert Cahn), Malzgasse 25, Tel. 237544. Coins and Greek vases are the firm's specialties. Dr. Cahn's annual auction sale, now in its fifteenth year, is a gathering place for collectors and museum curators the world over. Catalogs available by subscription.

George Zacos, 65 Engelgasse, Basel, Tel. 419638. By appointment only. Classical, ancient Near Eastern, and Byzantine art.

Lucerne

Ars Antiqua A.G. (Dr. Roland Maly), Haldenstrasse 5, Tel. 24392. The firm maintains a stock of antiquities and publishes occasional price lists.

Adolph Hess A.G., Haldenstrasse 5, Tel. 24392. Noted coin dealers. Catalogs and auction lists available by subscription.

Zurich

Bank Leu and Co., A.G. (Dr. L. Mildenberg), Bahnhofstrasse 32. Quality Greek, Roman, and Byzantine coins.

Galerie Arete (H. Humbel), Brandschenkestrasse 6, Tel. 442521. A newcomer to the trade, specializing in Greek, Roman, and Etruscan minor arts.

Jeannette Brun, 119 Dufourstrasse, Tel. 247086. By appointment only. Broad general stock of classical antiquities in every price range.

Galerie für Antike Kunst (Heidi Vollmoeller), Limmatquai 16, Tel. 323103. Specializes in the minor arts, especially jewelry and glass.

Lugano

Ugo Donati (Pino Donati), Via Nassa 32, Tel. 22028. The son of the well-known Lugano dealer has inherited his father's taste and connections. The emphasis continues to be on marbles, but fine terra-cottas from South Italy and Sicily, as well as Greek and Italiote vases, were also available the last time I visited.

PERIODICAL AND MAGAZINE PUBLICATIONS
OF INTEREST TO THE COLLECTOR
OF ANCIENT ART

Archaeology

A membership fee of $15 to the American Institute of Archaeology (100 Washington Square East, New York, N.Y. 10003) entitles the collector to a choice of either the institute's professional publication, *American Journal of Archaeology,* which appears quarterly and contains articles of specialized interest, or the popular magazine *Archaeology.* The latter, likewise a quarterly publication, features articles by noted American and European scholars on unknown or little-known works of art and on excavations, usually accompanied by ample photographic documentation (including colorplates).

Antike Kunst

An international periodical edited in Switzerland and conceived particularly for the discriminating collector of classical art. Appears quarterly, with occasional supplementary volumes. Articles predominantly on works of Greek and Roman art by distinguished international scholars, in French, English, and German. Vereinigung der Freunde Antiker Kunst, Dr. Hans Hotz, Essigstrasse 50, Riehn/Basel, Switzerland. Subscription price: SFr. 30 per year (ca. $7.50).

Apollo

The leading "glossy" magazine publication featuring ancient art. Edited by Denys Sutton; monthly. *Apollo Magazine,* Davies Street, London W.1, England. Annual subscription price: $24 (U.S. and Canada), which includes postage. An important feature of *Apollo* magazine is its extensive advertisement section, which give an excellent over-all view of works of art currently available.

Index

DATE DUE	BORROWER'S NAME

Hoffmann   240427